HO

Books by David Halberstam

The Noblest Roman

The Making of a Quagmire

One Very Hot Day

The Unfinished Odyssey of Robert Kennedy

Ho

The Powers That Be

The Breaks of the Game

The Amateurs

The Reckoning

The Best and the Brightest

HO

by David Halberstam

ALFRED A. KNOPF NEW YORK

ISBN: 0-394-46275-0 (hardcover)

ISBN: 0-394-36282-9 (paperbound)

Library of Congress Catalog Card Number: 77-140708

Manufactured in the United States of America

9 8 7 6 5 4 3 2 1

IN MEMORY OF **Mert Perry,**

GOOD REPORTER, GOOD FRIEND,

AND FOR HIS WIFE, **Darlene,**

AND HIS DAUGHTER, **Mia**

CONTENTS

HO

1

THE COLONIAL LEGACY OF THE FRENCH

"Your garden had nothing but grass."

AN ERA HAD JUST ENDED for the French in Indochina in the summer of 1954, and an empire had fallen. Only the pain of recognition was left, the counting of the casualties, the repatriation of the prisoners, the sorting out of a shattered spirit. In Hanoi, in a bar where once the pride of the French officer corps had swaggered, mocked their enemy, drunk their last cognacs and boasted of the next day's battle, a French correspondent was having a farewell drink with some friends. Across the bar he noticed a famous captain of the paratroops, a man legendary for his courage and élan, a survivor—one of the few—of Dienbienphu, now repatriated. The journalist, Lucien Bodard, went over to talk to him. But it was not the same captain. His eyes were different; his look, thought Bodard, was that of a sleepwalker—there was a lack of focus.

"It was all for nothing," he was saying. "I let my men die for nothing."

No one interrupted him. He continued, "In prison camp the Viets told us they had won because they were fighting for an ideal and we were not. I told them about my paras at Dienbienphu. I told them how they fought. And they said, 'Heroism is no answer.'

"In prison camp we faced the reality of the Vietminh. And we saw that for eight years our generals had been struggling against a revolution without knowing what a revolution was. Dienbienphu was not an accident of fate, it was a judgment."

HE WENT HOME sadder, wiser, more bitter. For a brief time, there was peace in Indochina, and then, inevitably, history repeated itself, all its mistakes. Another white man came to the Indochinese mainland, sure once again of his values, his ideas, his mission, willing both to die and to kill for them.

The Americans came, and with them their great generals and diplomats. These famous men arrived at the airport in Saigon, where American television teams rushed forward to record their words. Their statements promised imminent victory. For the French it had always been *le dernier quart d'heure,* for the Americans it was the light at the end of the tunnel—victory was just around the corner. The enemy—Communist, despised—was faltering (only the voices of the weak-kneed pacifists in Paris and New York kept him going). The local population—one did not use the word "native" any more—was rallying to the cause; the Vietnamese had seen through the deceit and duplicity of the Communists. Time is on our side; a nodding of heads by the colonels and majors who had come with the generals. At the edge of the crowd at the airport, pushed back by the television teams, was a young

4

American reporter named Neil Sheehan, one of the few who had understood early; after all, he had heard the same speech many times from many famous men. He listened with a small smile and then turned to a friend and said, "Ah, another foolish Westerner come to lose his reputation to Ho Chi Minh."

WESTERNERS had always arrived in Indochina sure of themselves, proud, believing above all that that which they were about to do was good not only for themselves and their beloved homelands, but for the Vietnamese as well, like it or not. The first missionaries who went there had assured Paris that the French would be greeted not as conquerors but as "liberators and benefactors." And what could be more congenial for a potential conqueror than the sure knowledge that his conquest was in the greater interest of the conquered as well? The French, after all, had greater learning, a superior culture, a modern language and a modern society; they were bigger, their sanitary habits—could anything be more revealing?—were better. The French had modern ships, modern weapons, a modern organizational sense to fit their expansionism. It was the height of European expansionism, of the developed Western society that had mastered the available technology, restlessly and relentlessly spreading itself around the world. Powerful companies run by powerful men dominated the governments of Europe, and these companies demanded the raw materials for their expanding markets. Their markets' interests and the national interests of the European nations happily coincided—flags to be planted, minerals and raw materials to be plucked everywhere. Europeans reached out to Africa, Asia and the Middle East, areas far behind in economic and political development in the modern sense, areas where, in contrast to the highly centralized political development of Europe, one found a virtually tribal structure; these were nations divided from within, living in a feudal era. The strong became stronger; the weak nations could not compete against the harnessed technology of the white man.

The white man's ideology comfortably adapted to the expansionism. It was right; it was part of the civilizing process. These primitive people could not govern themselves. The experience would be good for them, though painful to the colonizer. For it would hurt him more than the colonized; it was, in Kipling's words, the white man's burden. He would uplift the poor brown and poor yellow, teach him better, cleaner, more modern ways (teach him to have one wife—that first). To this end the white man came armed with his religion, which was a fine, pure and strict religion compared with the permissive and pagan religions of the natives (the permissiveness proved the paganism). It would not be an easy task; there would be much backsliding, but that was the burden of the missionary, indeed the very hardship of it: the difficulty, the pain, that was the proof that it was God's work.

FEW PARTS OF THE GLOBE appeared more inviting to an imperialist nation than Indochina. It was rich beyond belief in agricultural products (indeed, a later generation of Caucasians explained their stay in Vietnam as a means of preventing an expansionist Communist China from having the Vietnamese rice bowl). It had raw resources and it appeared vulnerable to foreign arms, being a typically feudal nation, divided within itself. Yet its ferocious warriors had managed to stave off European colonization in the seventeenth and eighteenth centuries,

6

first from the Dutch, and then the English. But where economic imperialism was defeated, religious imperialism succeeded.

In the seventeenth century a Catholic mission headed by a French Jesuit priest was permitted in. Alexandre de Rhodes headed the mission, converting tens of thousands of Vietnamese to Catholicism and, equally important, translating into the Latin alphabet the Chinese ideograms used by the Vietnamese, a step which became vital to the modernizing of Vietnam. Vietnamese Catholics remained after the French mission was expelled, eventually to be caught in internal wars. It was to protect the Vietnamese Catholics from persecution that the French landed at Danang in 1856 and began the chapter of colonial rule which was to end with the rise of Ho Chi Minh and the Vietminh in 1946, culminating in the defeat of the French forces at Dienbienphu in May 1954.

THE FRENCH COLONIAL MILITARY MACHINE, organized, centralized, had little trouble with fragmented Vietnam. It was necessary for the French to subdue only the top of the structure. It was a rotting society that was becoming increasingly ready for an upheaval. The arrival of the Caucasians simply postponed an inevitable revolution from within against the mandarin class, and meant that when the revolution came it was directed against the foreigner as well as against the upper class. (In general, it was against the upper class; a few exceptions in the mandarin class sided with the Vietminh, but most were tied by class, financial, religious and psychological bonds to the French.) But the advent of the French intensified the revolutionary forces at work in Vietnam; it sharpened contrasts; the inequities grew greater as the French

7

rushed the Vietnamese into the modern world.

The French experience was typical of the colonial era, no better and no worse: the white man had all the privileges, and the colonized, none. Even the word "Vietnam" was declared illegal. The jobs, the power, belonged to the French. A Vietnamese could only serve them. If he hoped to rise, he could only do it by moving up in the French structure, under French rules and control, becoming, in the eyes of his compatriots, more French than Vietnamese—a Vietnamese responding to the French rather than to his own people.

Most positions of semiprivilege went to the Catholics; in French eyes they were the secure ones; they got what little education was available, and they prospered. Their compatriots looked down on them because they had sold out to the foreign interest, were tainted by the foreign touch, foreign money. It was the first of a series of misperceptions of Vietnam: the Westerner looked upon the Catholic Vietnamese as the good Vietnamese, better educated, better trained, more civilized than the others, a reflection of what the country might become. By contrast, the other Vietnamese seemed shiftless; they, in turn, became more and more embittered, unable to rise in their own country.

The Vietnamese were fragmented politically, their suspicions of one another as great as their fear and hatred of the foreigners. From the time of the French conquest on, there were sporadic reactions against the colonial rule—an abused Vietnamese lashing out against a particularly vicious colon: a group forming in one village and ambushing a French unit; local insurrections lasting two or three days—but largely their resentment was inarticulate. The French were white and seemed all-powerful, a formidable nation-at-arms, and the Vietnamese looked at them and believed the myth of white superiority; thus the resistance was frail.

And so the servants and the tame Vietnamese officials would tell their masters that, yes, the Vietnamese liked them and that, yes, colonialism was good for Vietnam. Since it was what the French wanted to hear, and since there seemed to be scant evidence to contradict it, and that from malcontents, and since it seemed to come not just from the loyal *nha ques* (the servants), but from the *best-educated* Vietnamese—why, they believed they were benefactors, believed they were welcome, believed that the Vietnamese thought themselves fortunate to be under French rule.

Occasionally, however, there would be a glimpse, a brief glimpse, of what the Vietnamese really thought and felt. Perhaps nothing reveals their subsurface mood so well as a single poem written in the late-nineteenth century by an anonymous Vietnamese for the mock funeral of Francis Garnier, an early French explorer and conqueror who had carried out military operations in the northern part of the country, where he was killed in an ambush in Hanoi in 1873:

We remember you
In the days of old.
Your eyes were blue, marine-blue,
Your nose pointed up to the sky.
Your buttocks comfortably lodged against the ass's back.
Your mouth whistled noisily to the dogs.
Your house was full of bottles and bottle fragments.
Your garden had nothing but grass.
You ventured into the village of the Red Face.
You meant to pacify the Black Flags*

* A pirate group of Chinese and some Vietnamese, which was operating in the Hanoi area and which resisted French encroachment.

So that the whole population of our country might live in
    peace.
Who could have anticipated the terrible outcome:
That they would end your life!
They brought your head with them.
They abandoned there your sorry body.
Today we tremblingly obey the court's order.
We come to present in your devotion the following offer-
    ings:
A bunch of bananas,
Half a dozen eggs.
We dare hope these gifts
Will feed you to fulfillment.
You will continue to lie there in eternal rest.
Oh, Oh!
Your sorry body.
Sons of bitches, those who killed you.

Thus if the anti-French, antiwhite feeling was submerged it existed nonetheless, deep and powerful, await-
ing only the proper catalyst at the proper time to bring
it to the surface and turn it into a political force. The
French thought they were helping the Vietnamese, by
building roads and improving communications—and it is
true that in many ways they were hastening Vietnam's
jarring entry into the modern world. Yet their very presence created severe problems. In precolonial Vietnamese
society, taxes had been low, landholdings had been small,
and there had been few rich people. Those who were rich
had heavy obligations—they were expected to give large
parties and banquets—and they did not necessarily stay
rich very long. Indeed, the Vietnamese liked to quote an
old Chinese proverb to describe their traditional life: "No
one stays rich for three generations. No one stays poor for
three generations."

The French changed that; they set heavy taxes and
soon there was the growth of loans and usury, and some

Vietnamese became very rich. The French concentrated their interests in a few areas, such as finance and the rubber plantations, leaving the landholdings to the upper-class Vietnamese, who began to accumulate massive properties at the expense of the peasants, who were living in unparalleled poverty in a land so extraordinarily rich. By the beginning of the French Indochina war, in the Tonkin area 62 percent of the peasantry owned less than one ninth of an acre and 30 percent owned less than one fourth of an acre.

There were other frustrations, too. As the French colonial service developed and grew in Indochina, it trained a generation of Vietnamese just enough to make them hunger for more, just enough to teach them the inequities of the system. It was into this era of frustration and exploitation and hardship that Ho Chi Minh was born in the early 1890s.

2

PEASANT, DISHWASHER, SOCIALIST, COMMUNIST 1890–1917

"He stares disdainfully at a thousand athletes,
And bows to serve as a horse to children."

HO CHI MINH was one of the extraordinary figures of this era—part Gandhi, part Lenin, all Vietnamese. He was, perhaps more than any single man of the century, the living embodiment to his own people—and to the world—of their revolution. He was an old Bolshevik and a founding member of the French Communist party (what could be more alien to the average Vietnamese peasant?); yet to most Vietnamese peasants he was the symbol of their existence, their hopes, their struggles, their sacrifices and their victories. (Even after Dienbienphu, when many people of North Vietnam became angry with the Communist regime, they were always careful to exclude Ho from their blame: the Communists were responsible for the bad things—Ho, Uncle Ho, for the good things.) He was a more senior member of the Communist world than Mao, and he grouped around him an impressive assemblage of brilliant young men; he went through revolution, war, postwar development and another war without the slightest touch of purge. The Vietnamese Communist party remained to a unique degree a constant, mainly (according to students of its history) because of the dominating quality of its leader, for he combined total commitment with both tactical and long-range political skill.

Yet to the population he was always the symbol they needed: he was the gentle Vietnamese, humble, soft-spoken, mocking his own position, always seen in the simplest garb, his dress making him barely distinguishable from the poorest peasant—a style that Westerners for many years mocked, laughing at the lack of trappings of power, of uniform, of style, until one day they woke up and realized that this very simplicity, this cult of simplicity, this capacity to walk simply among his own people was basic to his success. In contrast, wrote Graham Greene in 1956 about Ngo Dinh Diem, the American-sponsored leader in the South, "He is separated from the people by cardinals and police cars with wailing sirens and foreign advisers droning of global strategy when he should be walking in the rice fields unprotected, learning the hard way how to be loved and obeyed—the two cannot be separated . . ."

Time magazine, the purest expression of Christian capitalism, in 1948 referred to Ho contemptuously as "goat-bearded," a "Mongoloid Trotsky" and a "tubercular agitator who learned his trade in Moscow." * But it was that very same contempt—which every peasant in Vietnam felt from every Westerner—that would make him so

---

* The simplistic American view of Asians which *Time* magazine exemplified was applied to its Asian heroes like Bao Dai as well. Thus in October 1946: " 'You ask him kill bird,' said foxy little Annamite Louis Ko. 'He no like. He like kill big.' Press agent Louis was speaking of his master, tall, strapping, Paris-educated Bao Dai who once killed 10 elephants in three days and captured one single handed.' "

effective. This was Ho's great strength, the fact that he was a Vietnamese Everyman, and it was why he shunned monuments and marshals' uniforms and generals' stars, for he had dealt with powerful Westerners all his life, had surely been offered countless bribes by them, but he had chosen not to be like them, not to dress like them or live like them. Rather, he remained a Vietnamese, a peasant, a man like one's ancestors—pure, uncorrupted in a corrupting world, a man of the land and its simple virtues.

In a country where the population had seen leaders reach a certain plateau and then become more Western and less Vietnamese, corrupted by Western power and money and ways, and where, the moment they had risen far enough to do anything for their own people, immediately sold out to the foreigners, the simplicity of Ho was powerful stuff. The higher he rose, the simpler and purer Ho seemed, always retaining the eternal Vietnamese values: respect for old people, disdain for money, affection for children. In 1951 in the middle of the war he could close a meeting of the Vietnamese Communist party by telling the gathering: "About a revolutionary man and a revolutionary party, the great Chinese writer Lu-Hsun has this couplet:

He stares disdainfully upon a thousand athletes,
And bows to serve as a horse to children.

" 'Thousand athletes,' " he would then explain, "means powerful enemies like the French colonialists and the American interventionists, or difficulties and hardships. 'Children' means the peaceful masses of people, or deeds beneficent to the State and party."

By his leadership and brilliance, Ho helped transform an era. In the twenties and thirties, he was one of the chief verbal critics of colonialism, a lonely and usually ignored voice. In the fifties, he was responsible for putting together the political and military machinery that led an underdeveloped peasantry in a successful revolutionary war against a powerful Western nation—a war that ended not only the French dominance over Vietnam but the mystique of white supremacy and colored inferiority throughout the colonial world. It also jarred a generation of Westerners out of the basic confidence in their ideas and institutions; jarred them out of the automatic assumption that these were the best of all possible ideas, that it was only a matter of transplanting them from Europe and America, where they had flourished, and diligently applying them to Asia and Africa. What Ho set forth in his successful revolutionary war against the French and his war against the Americans had enormous impact on the West and on the underdeveloped world. And in the West the younger generation particularly would understand and sympathize with what Ho had done far more than their parents did. Indeed, even while America was fighting Ho's troops, the American paperback edition of his writings, *Ho Chi Minh on Revolution* would claim, "Written in prison, exile, and battle, this is the political bible followed by half the world."

Throughout the underdeveloped world, after Dienbienphu the North Vietnamese were treated with a special respect. They had fought their war and they had won; there was no mistake about that. Vietnam, a small nation, had confirmed all the things that Asians and Africans had long wanted to believe about Western vincibility, be it moral, physical or spiritual. (Few, after all, could identify with what Mao had done—China was too large, and Mao had simply defeated other Chinese.) But the North Vietnamese had defeated a great Western nation. They had done it by being braver, smarter and truer to their own cause.

Yet for all Ho's extraordinary importance, for all of the richness of his life and his position as a symbol of the rebellion of the poor colored against the rich Caucasian, curiously little was known about him in the West. To Bernard Fall he said in 1962, "So you are the young man who is so much interested in all the small details about my life." Fall: "Mr. President, you are, after all, a public figure and it certainly would not be a violation of a military secret to know whether you had a family or were in Russia at a given date." Ho: "Ah, but you know I'm an old man, a very old man. An old man likes to have a little air of mystery about himself. I like to hold on to my little mysteries. I'm sure you will understand that . . ." There had always been a question as to whether or not he had ever married. He sometimes seemed to delight in creating rumors that he had. One night in 1945 Ho took Harold Isaacs, an American journalist, to the home of a Vietnamese friend. During the evening the friend's children brought out a packet of drawings inscribed to Ho. He seemed embarrassed by the attention. "I'm all alone," he told Isaacs afterward, "no family, nothing . . . I did have a wife once . . ."

Much of his life was cloaked in the anonymity that any Asian possessed, as far as Westerners were concerned, at the turn of the century. But he had as well the additional anonymity that goes with an underground figure—staying one step ahead of the police of several nations, changing his name regularly (at one point it was believed that he had died in a Hong Kong jail), then returning to his own nation to lead an underground revolution, this time from the mountains, so that even his wartime acts and decisions were curiously private and secret. Even in the Communist world more is normally known about leaders; Tito, Stalin, Khrushchev, Mao—all had their cult of personality.

But Ho deliberately did not seek the trappings of power and authority, as if he were so sure of himself and his relationship to both his people and history that he did not need statues and bridges, books and photographs to prove it to him or them. One sensed in him such a remarkable confidence about who he was, what he had done, that there would be no problem communicating it to his people; indeed, to try to communicate it by any artificial means might have created doubts among them. His abstinence from his own cult was particularly remarkable in the underdeveloped world, where the jump from poor peasant to ruler of a nation in a brief span of time often proves very heady stuff and inspires more than the predictable quota of self-commemoration.

THE VIETNAM INTO WHICH HO WAS BORN IN 1890*was a bitter land; the French ruled, but they ruled by force alone. They had destroyed the pride and traditions of the Vietnamese; they devalued what the Vietnamese venerated. To the Vietnamese, France seemed a world of policemen, soldiers, customs officials, clerks, informers. And to those Vietnamese who were too indiscreet about prizing their Vietnamese heritage France was represented by the prison island of Poulo Condore (Con Son), a place where nationalists went to serve their terms and from which they did not always return.

Ho came from the province of Nghe Thinh in central Vietnam, an area far from the lush delta of the north and the even lusher one of the south. (By a somewhat Toynbeean rationale, other Vietnamese have always regarded southerners as lazy, inferior soldiers and indifferent leaders,

* Though there is controversy about the date, this is the year accepted by his government.

the feeling being that their life is too easy, the soil too rich, and that men who lead such an easy life cannot be trusted to make the ultimate sacrifice for their country.) Nghe Thinh, infertile, impoverished, was known for its scholars. That area of central Vietnam was a traditional seat of Vietnamese learning. The province of Nghe Thinh was one of the most densely populated areas of Vietnam (a family might have to make do with one fifth of an acre), which caused problems. How could a young man work the land when there was no land to work? Naturally, he had too much time on his hands, and so he studied and became a scholar, but becoming a scholar in those days meant becoming an angry, frustrated young man. Indeed, the area had a time-honored reputation as a breeding ground for the restlessness and dissatisfaction so many of them fashioned out of the combination of the toughness of the land and a lingering sense of the glorious heritage of the past. It was an unwritten rule at the court of Hué, the capital of Annam, that mandarins from Nghe Thinh not be given jobs in the central government. They were too radical, too unpredictable; they caused too much trouble.

Ho's father, Nguyen Sinh Huy, was in this radical tradition. There are few clear recollections of the life of Ho's father—far fewer than there should be—but the French journalist-scholar Jean Lacouture was able to interview Paul Arnoux, a *Sûreté* official whose job it was to keep watch on Annamese immigrants in Paris, and who later created the Indochinese *Sûreté*. "When I first went to Annam in 1907 the older scholars in Hué spoke of a man of great learning who was a mandarin in Ha Tinh Province. He was reputed to know as many Chinese characters as any man in Vietnam, where there were many who had this skill. His name was Nguyen Sinh Huy. A few months later this man was dismissed from his office. In some police reports he was accused of alcoholism, in others, of embezzlement. Rather minor failings, they were widespread in the administration and smilingly overlooked so long as the offenders were politically tame. In fact, Nguyen Sinh Huy was really fired for his nationalist sympathies and because he was one of those Annamese who refused to learn French in order not to 'ruin' his own language—a weak excuse for a scholar of his calibre. One of his sons was called Nguyen Tat Thanh; that was the future Nguyen Ai Quoc, the future Ho Chi Minh. Thus Ho's life began in an atmosphere of anger, bitterness, of hatred towards France . . ."

Nguyen Sinh Huy was in his own way a revolutionary for his time; his life was both an overt and silent protest against the French (what better way to protest the foreigner than to refuse to learn his language—thus he does not exist). He had participated in the Scholars' Revolt of 1885 and had helped propagandize the anticolonial writings of Phan Boi Chau, a nationalist who had helped sharpen anti-French sentiment with a famous report called *Letter from Abroad Written in Blood*.

Nguyen Sinh Huy was the son of peasants. He tended buffaloes and worked on a farm, finally marrying the owner's daughter and receiving as her dowry a tiny paddy and a straw hut. He continued to study, passed the exam in Chinese literature, and earned the title of *pho bang* (a minor doctoral degree). He seemed headed toward the typical mandarin life: a teaching post at Thanh Hoa, then a job in the ceremonial office of the Imperial Palace at Hué —pleasant little functionary jobs that make a man a little better off than most of his colleagues. But he was strong and independent and decided not to accommodate himself to the colonial system. He told his family that "being a mandarin is the ultimate form of slavery."

He was made a deputy prefect in Binh Khe, but his

restlessness became evident. His work clearly reflected his distaste for his superiors and he was eventually dismissed by the French. (This would of course affect his son: that the father was a scholar, a man of learning, and yet was virtually unemployable and at the mercy of the French, while someone else without his talent and intelligence who accommodated himself to the foreigners could prosper.)* Next, Nguyen Sinh Huy wandered all over the Indochina peninsula setting bones, telling historical tales, writing letters for people—a wise and respected traveling scholar.

His children grew up under his influence and, while he was away, under the influence of an uncle who was also a fierce nationalist. Not surprisingly, Ho's sister, who worked in a noncommissioned officers mess, stole weapons and was jailed for life. His brother Khiem, another intense but erratic nationalist, wrote a letter to Albert Sarraut, the Governor General, complaining about the terrible poverty in Nghe An. Khiem was always more restless than Ho; his revolutionary zeal was hampered by a taste for alcohol, and his revolutionary activity was thus limited. When Khiem died in 1950 Ho, living in the underground *maquis,* was unable to attend the funeral and sent the local villagers a telegram which reflected his particular modesty and sense of Vietnamese traditions: "The onus of public affairs has not allowed me to look after him during his illness or to attend his funeral today. I humbly apologize for this failure in brotherly devotion and beg you to forgive a son

* A Vietnamese I knew in 1963 in Saigon said of that period, "It was a matter of intelligence. If you were very bright the choices were quite terrible because the brighter you were the more you understood exactly what was happening to you, and you either accommodated yourself to them and played on their side, or you had to leave them and fight them, and either choice was quite terrible. It was much easier for the ordinary man of ordinary ability."

who has had to put affairs of state before family feelings. Chi Minh."

Ho's was a hard boyhood, but it was also a time when he saw and learned much. He encountered the hardships of the peasants, the inequities of life, the injustices inflicted on his family; daily he learned that most difficult of lessons, the difference between what life is supposed to be according to schoolbooks and poems and what it really is. This contrasted most sharply with the Caucasians, French and Americans, who were to be his great adversaries in the middle of the century. They were men who had come from a vastly different background, men who had lived through relative prosperity, who were middle-class or better, led largely painless lives, men who had excelled in politics and the military but who had overcome far fewer obstacles than someone of Ho's background. Most important, they were men who saw the world as it was said to be, who accepted things at face value, who saw the structure in Vietnam that Ho wanted to destroy as working and did not challenge its very basis.

In Ho's boyhood, nothing was as it was said to be. The feeling against the French was building all the time; the French were conscripting forced labor to build roads, the coolies were escaping and staying in homes of people like Ho and his neighbors. Again and again there were minor rebellions which flickered and then died—because of a betrayal, a lack of organization, a failure to carry through.

ONE OF THE GREAT INFLUENCES in Ho's home was that of Phan Boi Chau, the foremost nationalist of that era, a man who had been a friend of Nguyen Sinh Huy. Chau was a towering figure; in 1902 he had won the highest honors possible for a Vietnamese in the literary competition held every three years at Vinh. Then he was offered high positions by the French, but turned them down; he would not be a symbol of the willingness of talented Vietnamese to serve the French. ("In the beginning of their conquest," he wrote instead, "the French used honeyed words and great rewards to entice the Vietnamese. They offered high government positions and benefits of all sorts to make some of us into their hunting dogs.") Again and again the French offered him jobs plus bribes to work for them, or at least to remain silent. Always he refused. As Ho would be typical of the revolutionaries of a new era, Chau symbolized the patriots of the previous one, a transitional era from the old feudal Vietnam to the modern society. He realized that the old parochial politics would no longer work, that broad parties were needed, that Vietnam must be modernized, and that his people must understand the new science and technology. Because of this he was drawn to Japan, the Asian nation which was most modern, and which had also defeated the Russians. In 1905 he began what was to be essentially an exile's life by going there. From Japan he continued to write passionately, becoming an even more famous figure in exile, so famous that the French leveled the death penalty against him *in absentia*. Chau also encouraged young Vietnamese to come to Japan, and because of him it emerged as an exile center in the early twentieth century. Where he differed from the younger Ho was that he was essentially a man of the old order. He thought Vietnam could be modernized and liberated without a genuine political revolution, that it all could be done through a reformed monarchy. He had, after all, been a full-fledged patriot before the turn of the century, while the younger Ho would emerge as a full-scale revolutionary only *after* the Russian Revolution. It was a crucial difference.

As a friend of the Nguyen Sinh Huy family he had intensified the anti-French feeling, and had encouraged Huy and his family to go to Japan. But Ho's father urged his sons to study French, perhaps sensing that in their lifetime the real struggle with the colonial power would come and that they would be better off if they knew as much as possible about France, its language and traditions.

This was a crucial decision for the embryonic revolutionary, for rather than taking his revolutionary guidance from China or Japan, learning their traditions and their politics, he would decide to spend his early days in Europe absorbing Western traditions and vulnerabilities, sharing experiences with left-wing Europeans, which inevitably brought him into the orbit of the young revolutionaries of the Soviet Union as that revolution was being exported. It also meant that in his speeches there would always be a strong sense of Western political heritage—homage to the French Revolution and the American Declaration of Independence—as if he were saying, "All right, you propagated these ideas, now we are trying to make good on them." One legacy is the fact that references to racial hatred seldom appeared in his speeches and decisions (there was a brief time in his Paris days when he signed himself Nguyen O Phap—Nguyen Who Hates the French); rather, there was a quiet admiration for the best of Westerners and their traditions, despite the fact that for most of his adult life he fought the West. Indeed, an official government book published in Hanoi explaining Ho's Western orientation says: "What attracts [Ho] to these [Western] countries is their ideology of freedom, of the sovereignty of the people, of democracy, of science and technology. He thought that to fight the French colonialists with the help of the Japanese militarists would be to 'hunt the tiger only to be eaten by the wolves.'" Thus Ho's family did not follow Phan Boi Chau to Japan. But Ho did listen particularly carefully to one bit of advice from the old nationalist: to be successful against the French, you will need a strong party, an organization in the real sense of the word.

Even before he was ready for school Ho was carrying messages for the anti-French underground. His father subsequently enrolled him in the French lycée in Vinh, but it was an arrangement which proved to be mutually unsatisfactory and he was soon expelled. The school officials said that the reason was poor grades; his friends said the reason was politics. His father then enrolled the teen-aged Ho at the Lycée Quoc-Hoc in the old imperial capital of Hué. The school was unique in that it blended modern French education with Vietnamese culture.

Ho's nationalist feeling was strengthened at Hué, which was a great center of learning, and where the feeling that the great culture of Vietnam was being crushed by the coarse, alien presence of the French was particularly strong.* The school at Hué became a training ground for many of the men who would serve as Ho's lieutenants in the fight against the French. While there, Ho continued to be active in nationalist affairs and he finally left the school without a diploma. It had not been a particularly happy or successful time, and he was a man who would learn more by making his own special odyssey through the outside world than by studying in the far more rigid world of the French-sponsored classroom.

For a while he taught in the fishing village of Phan

* In the 1963 Buddhist riots against the government of South Vietnam the reaction was particularly intense in Hué, where there was a feeling that the Catholic-dominated government of the Ngo family was depriving Buddhism of its traditional rights and prerogatives; a Catholic, Western-oriented government seemed far more alien when viewed from Hué than from Saigon.

Thiet, badly paid like all teachers of that time, and shortly afterward he went to Saigon to learn a trade. There is some difference of opinion about what trade he actually studied (it is indicative of the many shadows in Ho's career that there is a difference of opinion on almost every major fact in his life: his date of birth, his father's name, his own name, whether he ever married, etc.). Some believe he intended to study seamanship; Bernard Fall believed he studied cooking, since it was probably the easiest way for a Vietnamese to find a well-paying job, and since it was not as demeaning as some of the other possibilities.

Then, in 1912, at the age of twenty-two, he decided to leave Vietnam for the West, to study the European world. Some French and Americans would later be puzzled as to how Ho, after spending so many years outside of Vietnam, could return to become such an immediately viable political force in his native land. The reason is that these were the right years to be out of Vietnam. Only by not being there could a Vietnamese have the full freedom to say what he felt, and what his countrymen longed to hear. In the vacuum of Vietnamese leadership of those years the clear and consistent voice of Ho had great impact among younger Vietnamese. In contrast, in 1954 the Americans helped install Ngo Dinh Diem in the South, unmindful of the fact that he had been out of the country during the French-Indochina war. To the Americans this was the most attractive part—he was anti-Communist but had not been tainted by being pro-French. But to most Vietnamese these were the wrong years to be out of Vietnam—he was already disqualified from serious consideration as a patriot because he had been out of the country, *un attentiste*, during the most important period in Vietnamese history, a period that separated the men from the boys. In addition, Diem was at a tactical disadvantage, for that revolutionary time with its extraordinary sense of ferment and excitement had changed the entire style of Vietnamese political life. Now everything was possible, but Diem was still living in the past. He believed in a mandarin age which had ended the moment the French-Indochina war had begun. Diem was intent on being above all the good mandarin, not knowing that from 1946 on there could be no good mandarins left in Vietnam.

HO BEGAN HIS TRAVELS as a mess boy on the French liner *Latouche-Tréville*. He spent two years aboard the ship, touring all the ports of Africa and Europe. In Africa he saw that what applied to the French colonialism he knew also applied in other colonies, that the problems for the Vietnamese were the same as for the blacks. His travels took him all over the globe and probably to America. Every time he saw Americans he asked questions which implied that he knew their country very well. It is even believed that Ho lived for a brief time in Harlem, but it is one of those points in his life that remain something of a mystery.

He finally left the ship to work in England during World War I. He was a pastry cook for the famous Escoffier at the Carlton Hotel, living the darkest and poorest kind of life while working in the plushest kitchen and serving the richest people in the world. At this time he also had his first contact with exiled Asians, joining the Lao Dang Hoi Nagai (Overseas Workers), a Chinese-dominated group of Asian expatriates. He also studied the Irish uprising and talked with some of the Fabians, but he was restless in England: it seemed that the real problems of his own country could be addressed from only two places, Vietnam or France. So he went to France in 1917, the worst and darkest days of the war.

Now for the first time he had contact with people in metropolitan France and found their behavior and beliefs quite different from the French he had met in the colonies. It was as if they were two different breeds: the right-wing, race-conscious Frenchmen who served their nation overseas, and the other French at home, far less prejudiced. All around him during this period he saw the deprivation of the average French workingman, and it was a revelation: before, all Frenchmen were rich and powerful, all Asians weak and poor. Now he was looking at frightened and hungry Frenchmen, and they seemed less aware of racial distinctions. "He was," wrote Jean Lacouture, "struck by the similarity between the lot of the exploited inhabitant of a colony and that of a European worker—and it was to this parallel . . . that he was to devote one of his earliest articles. No one could have felt more naturally drawn to organized labor and the parties of the left. Had he stayed at home, he might never have progressed beyond an extremist form of nationalism, without ideological perspective and concerned exclusively with evicting the foreign invader—a form of nationalism perhaps even tinged with racism, as in the case of the Phu Quoc movement. Living immersed for a while in a hierarchical, industrialized society broadened his outlook and gave a political slant to his thought. Contact with the French Left was soon to turn an angry patriot into a modern revolutionary. The colonial system had made him a stranger in his own country; the French in France were to make him a fellow citizen."

The early years in Paris were difficult ones. He was a poor man trying to find his way in a poor and stricken nation, but he had already charted his course: he would be a revolutionary. First, however, he needed a name. Since leaving Vietnam he had simply been known as Ba. Now he chose a new name: Nguyen Ai Quoc. Nguyen in Vietnam is the equivalent of Smith or Jones in America. Quoc means "country," so his name really meant Nguyen the Patriot. He would go by this name for years, as a writer, in the Comintern records, and of course in various police dossiers.

The Chinese calligraphy he had studied as a child was for the first time of value as he began to earn a small living using his manual skill in photo retouching. The Socialist party newspaper *La Vie Ouvrière* in 1918 carried a small classified advertisement saying: "You who would like a living remembrance of your relatives, have your photographs retouched by Nguyen Ai Quoc. Handsome portraits and handsome frames for 45 francs . . ." But these were not days when poor Frenchmen were beating down doors to have their photographs taken, let alone retouched, and there was little money in this occupation. He was impoverished, often hungry, usually unemployed, often at odds with the police. His inability to pay his rent sent him from apartment to apartment.

Although this was a difficult time economically, it was an exciting time politically. The war was destroying the old structure of society; no one knew what the new one might be. One heard stories from Moscow, where the Bolsheviks had seized power. Might all of Europe soon be like this? Like other cities, Paris seethed with talk, with late-night discussions among left-wing intellectuals.

Ho was a part of this world. He surrounded himself with other Vietnamese revolutionaries, met with radical workers, frequented a bookshop which Leon Trotsky himself reputedly had visited from time to time. Ho met trade union officials, pacifists, wrote articles for *L'Humanité* under the title "Reminiscences of an Exile" and wrote a political play called *The Bamboo Dragon* (said to be so bad that it is not even performed in Hanoi). He met Marx's grandson, and he became the first Vietnamese member of the Young Socialists. Another Vietnamese who knew him at the time but who later became a bitter anti-Communist described Ho as a "wraithlike figure always armed with a book—who read Zola, France, Shakespeare, Dickens, Hugo, and Romain Rolland. He became friends with an old anarcho-syndicalist militant, Jules Raveau, who had recently returned from Switzerland, where he had been working with Lenin and Zinoviev . . . intimately associated with the Bolshevik group, he was for Ho an unfailing source of information, guidance and anecdotes. [Raveau] was for a long time an adviser to the young Annamese, who as a result became a regular visitor to the tiny editorial office of *La Vie Ouvrière*, in the district of Belleville, where there was a powerful revolutionary tradition. Tales of the men and women of the Commune who were slaughtered by M. Thiers' soldiers and now lay in Père Lachaise cemetery merged in the young man's mind with memories of uprisings staged by his own countrymen."

Ho was already becoming a figure of some prominence in the left-wing world of Paris, and French *Sûreté* officials began to keep an eye on him. Paul Arnoux, the *Sûreté* man who watched over the Vietnamese community, went one evening to hear one of Ho's compatriots plead the cause of Vietnamese independence, but he was far more interested in a small Asian standing by the door handing out leaflets advocating violence. This, Arnoux was told, was Nguyen Ai Quoc. Arnoux had often heard of him and arranged a meeting with him, the first of several. Arnoux was taken with Ho, with his intensity. Ho would talk of his country and what the French had done to his people, and particularly to his father. "France," he would say,

"France was the villain." Arnoux, impressed by his passion and intelligence—a young man to keep an eye on—suggested that Albert Sarraut, minister for colonial affairs, meet him. But Sarraut was dubious; he even doubted whether there was such a person as Nguyen Ai Quoc. Instead, Ho finally met an underling, but little came of it. Indeed a few years later, when Ho felt himself under increasing police surveillance he wrote an article in an anticolonial newspaper to which he contributed regularly, *Le Paria* (The Outcast), mocking the police watch:

> But "keeping-watch" alone seemed to Your Excellency's fatherly solicitude insufficient and you wanted to do better. That is why for some time now you have granted each Annamese—dear Annamese, as Your Excellency says— private aides-de-camp. Though still novices in the art of Sherlock Holmes, these good people are devoted and particularly sympathetic. We have only praise to bestow on them and compliments to pay their boss, Your Excellency. . . . If Your Excellency insists on knowing what we do every day nothing is easier: we shall publish every morning a bulletin of our movements, and Your Excellency will have but the trouble of reading. Besides our timetable is quite simple and almost unchanging.
> Mornings: from 8 to 12 at the workshop.
> Afternoons: in the newspaper offices (leftist, of course) or at the library.
> Evenings: at home or attending educational talks.
> Sundays and holidays: visiting museums or other places of interest.
> There you are!—Nguyen Ai Quoc.

The world around him was in turmoil. The Communist seizure of power in Russia had had a potent effect on the exile community. In addition, thought Ho and his colleagues, perhaps there was hope from the new colossus of the West. America had entered the war belatedly, and now, in January 1918, Woodrow Wilson, her almost evangelical President, who spoke of freedom for all, of self-determination for all peoples, was crossing the Atlantic armed with his moral grandeur and his Fourteen Points; he was coming to put an end to war and all of mankind's suffering. Ho, more and more the leader of the Vietnamese group in Paris, prepared his own eight-point program for freedom in Vietnam, based on Wilson's Fourteen Points.

In retrospect it seems to have been a moderate program: the Vietnamese wanted representation in the French parliament, freedom of the press, freedom to hold meetings and form groups, release of political prisoners and amnesty for them, government by law instead of decree, and equal rights for Vietnamese and French. Modest requests, though, of course, if granted they would have soon made independence a reality: for they would have released all the pent-up longings in the country and it would have been impossible to stop the pressure for independence. Wilson was determined to bring a just peace and self-determination to nations yet unborn, but it was still a white man's world. Democracy was something for white nations; a nation yet unborn meant a European nation yet unborn; and besides, France was a great ally of the Americans.

In 1919 Ho and his group had their eight-point program carefully printed (though the printer misspelled Ho's name) and he set off for Versailles, where representatives of the underdeveloped world were crowded, all trying to gain a hearing, demanding their independence, their boundaries restored. But the great powers at Versailles never heard Ho (the official records nowhere indicate that a petition for Vietnamese independence was even under consideration). Ho and the other petitioners at Versailles reacted bitterly among themselves. The moderate solution they had sought was no longer viable, the great powers understood only power; and for a small country, power meant armed revolution, terrorism, bombs and guns. To sit and make nice genteel requests which should be honored in a nice genteel way was pointless— one was only brushed aside. Ho's appearance at Versailles had made no impression on the great figures there, nor on the Western press. In the Western field of vision he did not exist.

But in the world of the Paris-based Vietnamese his very failure there had enhanced his position. It was Ho who had represented them at Versailles and tried to put forward their position; it was Ho, and thus all Vietnamese, that the great men had rejected. In the growing semi-underground world of the Vietnamese community in France, Ho had become The Figure; Bui Lam, a student in Paris at the time, later recollected (in an official North Vietnamese publication): ". . . no two Vietnamese residing in France could meet after this without mentioning the name of Nguyen Ai Quoc." Now as Vietnamese arrived in France they were drawn to him, guided by him. He wandered through the industrial quarters of Paris talking to workers, seeking out the students, the young, telling them they must be involved—"Your studies can wait—come and work with us."

IN DECEMBER 1920 the French Socialist party held a crucial meeting in the city of Tours. It was a great galaxy of French left-wing figures. Ho felt awed by the intellectual brilliance around him—the flashing debate with minor points representing major political schisms, much of the discussion touching on subtleties far removed from his own single-minded purpose: he was a Socialist so that Vietnam could be free. That single-mindedness came through in his own speeches, and with it some of his doubts even about these French colleagues, so much more sympathetic to him and his cause than most Caucasians. Yet perhaps he sensed that sympathy was not enough. Perhaps the feeling of urgency and the totality of commitment that his own cause demanded were lacking among these intelligent, liberal, humane men, so concerned with their own special grievances against the capitalist system. They wanted more for the workers, but did they go far enough? Would they perhaps be willing to continue the same exploitation of the yellow man, provided the white worker had a fairer share of the pie? Was it only lip-service sympathy, too genteel for the harsher commitment that reality demanded? His speech is still recorded:

Chairman: Comrade Indochinese Delegate, you have the floor.

Indochinese Delegate [Nguyen Ai Quoc]: Today, instead of contributing, together with you, to world revolution, I come here with deep sadness to speak as a member of the Socialist Party, against the imperialists who have committed abhorrent crimes on my native land. You all have known that French imperialists entered Indochina half a century ago. In its selfish interest it conquered our country with bayonets. Since then we have not only been oppressed and exploited shamelessly, but also tortured and exploited pitilessly . . . Prisons outnumber schools and are always overcrowded with detainees. Any natives having socialist ideas are arrested and sometimes murdered without trial. Such is the so-called justice in Indochina. In that country, the Vietnamese are discriminated against, they do not enjoy safety like Europeans or those having European citizenship. We have neither freedom of the press nor freedom of speech. Even freedom of assembly and freedom of association do not exist. We have no right to live in other countries or to go abroad as tourists. We are forced to live in utter ignorance and obscurity because we have no right to study . . . Comrades, such is the treatment inflicted upon more than 20 million Vietnamese, that

33

is more than half the population of France. And they are said to be under French protection! The Socialist Party must act realistically to support the oppressed natives.

Jean Longuet: I have spoken in favor of the natives [i.e. we are doing our part, what more can we do?].

Indochinese Delegate: Right from the beginning of my speech I have already asked everyone to keep absolute silence. The party must make propaganda for socialism in all colonial countries. We have realized that the Socialist Party's joining the Third International means that it has practically promised that from now on it will correctly assess the importance of the colonial question. We are very glad to learn that a Standing Delegation has been appointed to study the North African question, and, in the near future, we will be very glad if the Party sends one of its members to Indochina to study on the spot the questions relating to this country and the activities which should be carried out there.

[A right-wing delegate had a contradictory opinion, which angered Ho.]

Indochinese Delegate: Silence! . . .

Chairman: Now all delegates must keep silence! Including those not standing for the Parliament!

Indochinese Delegate: On behalf of the whole of mankind, on behalf of the Socialist Party's members, both left and right wings, we call upon you! Comrades, save us!

Again Longuet outlined the steps he had taken in Parliament on behalf of the colonized peoples, and this time a radical Frenchman got up to agree with Ho that "Parliament is not the only place where one must fight on behalf of the oppressed nations."

THE SPEECH AND THE MEETING marked the end of Ho the Socialist. He had realized, particularly after the brush-off at Versailles, that harsh measures would be required to free Vietnam from French rule. But would these measures be forthcoming from these Socialists, with their humane tradition, their fondness for parliamentary action? They were good men, but did they go far enough? Did they reject the system, or did they simply want to change the balance a little? Were they too willing to compromise, more bourgeois than they realized, "capitalist souls in syndicalist bodies," as one opponent called them? This was not a small happenstance conflict but a deep schism that touched on one of the basic issues which would divide the left throughout the contemporary world: at what point does injustice merit violence? If one seeks justice and liberty, does this give one the right to strike out with antidemocratic, indeed violent measures? The French Socialist party split after Tours, and on December 30 the French Communist party was founded. Ho was one of the founding members.

FROM BELIEF TO PROFESSION: HO'S PATH TO COMMUNISM 1917–1940

"The radical sun illuminating our path."

HISTORY SETS OFF ITS OWN CHAIN REACTIONS; one great event touches off another. That there would one day be revolution against the white man in Vietnam was inevitable, but the timetable was not fixed. World War I had come, leaving in its bitter wake a Communist Russia and an exhausted and decaying Europe. The aftereffects of that war would lead to the next war and see China become Communist. Ho's lifetime would span all these great events. History to a large degree would come his way, and when it did he would not be caught unprepared. He had arrived in Europe a young and virtually nameless refugee at a time when the old order had seemed secure on the surface, when the great powers were simply involved in traditional rivalries—a border conflict here, a sphere of influence there, an outbreak of chauvinism here, all culminating in World War I; out of that war would come new alignments and a breakdown of the old order. And he himself would be no immobile bystander; rather, his own life would be a key factor in affecting changes that would see the old order in ruins and the West learning the limits of power—that gunboat diplomacy and colonialism were finished.

As a young Socialist-turned-Communist, Ho was drawn to the Russian experience and Lenin. Paul Mus, the distinguished French scholar, said of him: "He became a Leninist, since Lenin was faced in Russia with the same problem of the vacuum at the village level. Ho was successful because he remained true to Leninism and Marxism. In this sense, straightforward according to *his* view, he belongs to a proper fraternity." Not just ideology, not just words; he had heard enough words, all of them brilliant, each critique more incisive than the last. Here was action and, more important, success. The Bolsheviks had done it; blood had flowed, yes, but they had won. They had not only talked revolution, they had carried it out. They had brought the right organization, the right structure, the right ideology at the right time. They were violent; well, the times required violence. Based on his experience at the Tours meeting, Ho knew that they had been without illusion about the price, and they had paid it. They were the model (they had not, after all, been in power long enough to start failing, to form their own bureaucracy). Ho's writings in the twenties and thirties again and again reflected his homage to Lenin (in a way that they would not for Stalin), and in 1960, in one of the clearest explanations of his own ideological course, he wrote an article entitled "The Path Which Led Me to Leninism":

> After World War I, I made my living in Paris, now as a retoucher at a photographer's, now as a painter of "Chinese antiquities" (made in France!). I would distribute leaflets

denouncing the crimes committed by the French colonialists in Vietnam.

At that time I supported the October Revolution only instinctively, not yet grasping all its historic importance. I loved and admired Lenin because he was a great patriot who liberated his compatriots; until then I had read none of his books.

The reason for my joining the French Socialist Party was that these "ladies and gentlemen"—as I called my comrades at that moment—had shown their sympathy toward me, toward the struggle of the oppressed peoples. But I understood neither what was a party, a trade union, nor what was Socialism or Communism.

Heated discussions were then taking place in the branches of the Socialist Party about the question of whether the Socialist Party should remain in the Second International, should a Second-and-a-half International be founded, or should the Socialist Party join Lenin's Third International? I attended the meetings regularly twice or three times a week and attentively listened to the discussions. First I could not understand thoroughly. Why were the discussions so heated? Either with the Second, Second-and-a-half or Third International the revolution could be waged. What was the use of arguing, then? As for the First International, what had become of it?

What I wanted to know most—and this precisely was not debated in the meetings—was: Which International sides with the peoples of colonial countries?

I raised this question—the most important, in my opinion—in a meeting. Some comrades answered, "It is the Third, not the Second International." And a comrade gave me Lenin's "Thesis on the National and Colonial Questions," published by *L'Humanité*, to read.

There were political terms difficult to understand in this thesis. But by dint of reading it again and again, finally I could grasp the main part of it. What emotion, enthusiasm, clear-sightedness and confidence it instilled in me! I was overjoyed. Though sitting alone in my room I shouted aloud as if addressing large crowds: "Dear martyrs, compatriots! This is what we need, this is our path to liberation!"

After that I had full confidence in Lenin, in the Third International.

Formerly during the meetings of the Party branch I only listened to the discussions; I had a vague belief that all were logical, and could not differentiate as to who was right and who was wrong. But from then on I also plunged into the debates, and discussed with fervor. Though I still lacked French words to express all my thoughts, I smashed the allegations attacking Lenin and the Third International with no less vigor. My only argument was: "If you do not condemn colonialism, if you do not side with the colonial people, what kind of revolution are you waging? . . .

At first patriotism, not yet Communism, led me to have confidence in Lenin, in the Third International. Step by step, along the struggle, by studying Marxism-Leninism parallel with participating in practical activities I gradually came upon the fact that only Socialism and Communism can liberate the oppressed nations and the working people throughout the world from slavery.

There is a legend in our country, as well as in China, on the miraculous "Book of the Wise"! When facing great difficulties, one opens it and finds a way out. Leninism is not only a miraculous "book of the wise," a compass for us Vietnamese revolutionaries and people: it is also the radiant sun illuminating our path to final victory, to Socialism and Communism.

Now Ho turned from the ideologist and the young student rebel into the real revolutionary—he went from belief and feeling to profession. He founded the Inter-colonial Union in 1921 as a Communist front, and he wrote consistently for his paper, *Le Paria*. There he repeatedly attacked the entire structure of French colonialism and offered weekly praise to Moscow, the new center of his universe.

Typically, he wrote: "One day a native clerk left work reading a novel. Coming to an amusing passage, the reader began to laugh. Just then he passed Mister

Overseer of Public Works and the latter flew into a rage, first of all because the native, absorbed in his reading, hadn't noticed him and greeted; secondly because the native had taken the liberty of laughing as he passed a white man. Our civilizer therefore stopped the Annamese and after asking his name, asked if he wanted a slap in the face. Naturally the clerk declined the far too generous offer and expressed surprise at such a storm of abuse. Without more ado the official grabbed the native by the jacket and dragged him before the head of the province . . ." Another story went: "A customs clerk obliged natives passing by his house to doff their hats or get off their mounts. One day this civilizer brutalized an Annamese woman, who though she had greeted him, had forgotten to call him Great Mandarin. This woman was pregnant. A violent kick right in the stomach aimed by the agent caused a miscarriage; the unfortunate woman died shortly after . . ."

But with the founding of the French Communist party his life had changed in a far more basic and important way. As Bernard Fall wrote: "From an isolated young man in a hostile community he was now a sought-after party official in a world-wide charismatic movement with the financial backing of a powerful state: the Soviet Union. Funds suddenly became available for more lecture trips inside France . . ." Among Asian exiles he became the man to see, to clear it with; he had access to other powerful men, to money. For a young Vietnamese angry about the French domination and anxious to join a movement to change it, suddenly the place to be was Paris, and the contact man was Ho."

In 1923 he began two extraordinary decades of travel and continuing exile. To Russia. Out of Russia. Into Western Europe; changed names, out again. Back to Asia (but not Vietnam). Then to Moscow again. In Moscow, hailed as an important and influential leader of an embryonic nation, then off again, no longer a leader hailed and honored but a shadowy figure living a semiclandestine life, changing hiding places, staying one step ahead of the police. "The colonialists will be on your trail," he advised one Vietnamese returning to the homeland, "keep away from our friends' houses and don't hesitate to pose as a degenerate if it will help put the police off the scent . . ."

Sometimes he fell one step behind the police, ending up in jail, be it a British one in Hong Kong or a Nationalist one in China. (While in jail he wrote one of his best poems about the contrast between his reception in China and that of the American politician Wendell Willkie: "Both of us are friends of China/ Both are going to Chungking/ But you are given the seat of an honored guest/ While I am a prisoner thrown under the steps/ Why are we both so differently treated?/ Coldness to one, and warmth toward the other:/ That is the way of the world, as from time immemorial/ The waters flow down to the sea.") During all that time he was setting up the first stages of the political organization that would culminate with the formation of the Vietminh, a task which involved not so much finding eager recruits as preventing the various factions of radical left-wing groups from destroying each other in typically Vietnamese fratricidal strife.

HO APPARENTLY STAYED IN PARIS throughout most of 1923, doing a good deal of writing for *Le Paria*, and then went to Moscow for the first time shortly after the death of Lenin. (In January 1924 *Pravda* published an article by Ho on the death of Lenin: "Lenin is dead. What are we going to do? That is the question the oppressed masses in the colonies are anxiously asking themselves . . .") To a Japanese friend Ho suggested in late November that they go to Moscow together, "the birthplace of revolution." The Japanese answered that he preferred to study art and literature and therefore would remain in Paris. "What kind of art can you practice in this rotten society?" Ho demanded. "We will make the revolution, and then you can write for the free men in a classless society."

He spent 1924 in the Soviet Union, taking courses at the University of the Peoples of the East, writing for *Pravda* and other Soviet publications. Ruth Fischer, the German Communist representative in the Comintern, recalled Ho at that time:

> When he first arrived he seemed very inconsequential. He had neither the dash nor the presence of that other Asian revolutionary, the Indian leader Roy. But he immediately won the respect and even the affection of us all. Amid these seasoned revolutionaries and rigid intellectuals, he struck a delightful note of goodness and simplicity. He seemed to stand for mere common decency—though he was cleverer than he let on—and it was his well-earned good name which saved him from getting caught up in internal conflicts. Also, he was temperamentally far more inclined towards action than towards doctrinal debates. He was always an empiricist within the movement. But none of this detracted from his colleagues' regard for him, and his prestige was considerable. He played a very big part in things, bigger than some of the better-known Asian leaders of the time—Mao did not come to the fore till later.

During this period Ho was interviewed by the famous poet Osip Mandelstam, now regarded as one of the most significant poets of modern Russia. Mandelstam, who later died a terrible death during the worst of Stalin's purges, published his interview in *Ogonek* in a December 1923 issue. Part of the article follows:

"And how has Gandhi's movement been reflected in Indochina? Haven't any of the reverberations, any echoes, reached there?" I asked Nguyen Ai Quoc.

"No," answered my companion. "The Annamese people —peasants—live buried in the profoundest night, with no newspapers, no conception of what's happening in the world. It's night, actual night."

Nguyen Ai Quoc is the only Annamese in Moscow and represents an ancient Malaysian race. He is practically a boy, thin and lithe, wearing a knitted woolen jacket. He speaks French, the language of the oppressors, but the French words sound dim and faint, like the muffled bell of his native language.

Nguyen Ai Quoc utters the word "civilization" with disgust: he has travelled the length and breadth of practically the whole colonial world, been in northern and central Africa and he's seen his fill of it. In conversation he often uses the word "brothers." His "brothers" are the Negroes, Hindus, Syrians, Chinese. . . .

"I come from a privileged Annamese family. In my country such families don't do anything. The young men study Confucianism. You know, Confucianism is not a religion, but rather a study of moral practice and decent behavior. In its very foundation it presupposes a 'social world.' I was a boy of about thirteen when I first heard the French words for liberty, equality and fraternity . . . And I wanted to learn something about French civilization to explore what lay concealed behind those words. But the French are training parrots in the native schools. They hide books and newspapers from us, and ban not only modern writers but even Rousseau and Montesquieu . . ."

I had a vivid image of the way these gentle people, with their love for tact and moderation and their hatred of excess, had been made to drink hard liquor. Nguyen Ai Quoc's whole presence was imbued with an innate tact and delicacy. European civilization works with bayonet and liquor, hiding them under the soutane of a Catholic missionary. Nguyen Ai Quoc breathes culture, not European culture, but perhaps the culture of the future . . .

"Yes, it's interesting how the French authorities taught our peasants the words 'Bolshevik' and 'Lenin'! They began hunting down Communists among the Annamese peasantry at a time when there wasn't a trace of a Communist. And that way they spread the propaganda."

The Annamese are a simple courteous people. In the nobility of his manner and in the dim soft voice of Nguyen Ai Quoc one can hear the approach of tomorrow, the oceanic silence of universal brotherhood. There's a manuscript on the table. A calm, businesslike report. The telegraphic style of a correspondent. He's indulging his fancy on the theme of a Congress of the International in the year 1947. He sees and hears the agenda, he's present, taking down the minutes . . .

Sometime in late 1924 or early 1925 Ho was sent from Moscow to Canton by the leaders of the International to assist Mikhail Borodin, the Comintern envoy to the new Chinese revolutionary government; he was assigned as both interpreter and political adviser. Canton was a great center for Vietnamese exile politics; thus Ho could meet readily with young compatriots who had slipped over the border into China. In Vietnam it was a time of constant abortive incidents, all stirring powerful feelings in the population, but all fizzling out. A bomb had been thrown at the Governor General; the episode created a good deal of excitement, which soon died down, however. Ho realized that it would take a tough-structured organization to achieve success.

The old Vietnamese nationalist Phan Boi Chau, the friend of Ho's father, was in Canton, where he had attracted a considerable circle of young Vietnamese exiles. Now a militant, Moscow-trained professional, Ho regarded Phan Boi Chau as something of a disappointment and a problem; he was a relic of the past. He seemed not a revolutionary but a somewhat parochial protester against the status quo; to Ho's group Phan seemed a man too content to sit and talk when the world was changing and the times called for action. One of Ho's associates came up with an idea which would provide the revolutionary groups with some funds and at the same time increase nationalist fervor inside Vietnam. He suggested to Ho that Chau, the most famous of the leaders in Canton be sacrificed to the national cause. By selling Chau out to the French they would get a reward, while the arrest and trial would arouse the Vietnamese people and bring international attention. International feeling would be so strong that they would not be able to bring the death sentence against Chau. Ho agreed, and in June 1925 Chau received an invitation to attend a special meeting of Vietnamese revolutionaries. As he arrived in Shanghai, he was grabbed by a group of strangers and taken to a French office and from there to Hanoi. It is believed that Ho's intermediary received 150,000 piasters from the French. Chau was tried, given a life sentence of hard labor, and pardoned a few weeks later; the French Governor General then invited Chau to spend a night at the residence but the old patriot refused even then to cooperate with the colonialists.

He was removed, however, from the political scene, and in Canton Ho was quickly able to pick up some of the young exiles who had gathered around Chau, and there started his own group. To the younger men who had already become impatient with what they considered the vagueness and softness of Chau's policies, Ho, fresh from Moscow with his new credentials and training, seemed an attractive alternative. With five young Vietnamese he organized the Association of Vietnamese Revolutionary Youth, or Thanh Nien (so called after its newspaper), a group which eventually became the forerunner of the Indochinese Communist party. "*Thanh Nien* did not immediately appear to be a Marxist sheet and the topics it dealt with were primarily nationalistic," writes Lacouture, "but the authors subtly incorporated some of the basic terms and expressions of Leninist dialectics in the attempt to pave the way for the 'second phase' of the revolution. For Ho knew well enough that the audience he must reach consisted, in the main, of tradition-bound peasants. Therefore he had deliberately divided his campaign into two stages: the first was basically national, appealing to the 'most conscientious elements in every class' with a view to establishing a 'bourgeois-democratic' regime; the second led to socialism only after a transformation of economic and social conditions that might take several decades . . ."

DESPITE THE ARREST OF PHAN BOI CHAU, Ho had not, by 1925, removed all opposition among the nationalists; indeed there was considerable suspicion of him and his Moscow origins in some of the other fledgling groups, several of them more parochial and upper-class oriented. Some of the secret societies which had followed Phan Boi Chau now broke off and formed a group called the Tan Viet. Ho's group flirted with this new group and hoped to absorb it. But the Tan Viet leaders were dubious, and in 1927, in an attempt to keep from being absorbed by the Communists, they joined forces with another party. This was the Viet Nam Quoc Dan Dang or VNQDD (Vietnam Nationalist party) somewhat similar to the Tan Viet in make-up (schoolteachers, functionaries) though somewhat more urban-oriented. It was particularly strong in the Hanoi area (there, someone like a schoolteacher could be quite effective, even though he could not travel as freely as a revolutionary should be able to).

The VNQDD was more sophisticated in political organization than any of its predecessors with their dependency upon the old secret societies. For the first time, a Vietnamese political party was able to get beyond its own parochialism. By 1929 it was also numerically the strongest party in Vietnam, with more than 1,500 persons belonging to 120 cells. At this point it decided on a program of public militancy to demonstrate that it was a powerful, growing force; by showing strength it would gain even more support and thus dominate the entire nationalist scene. It was a bold idea, and its failure was to redound to Ho's advantage as much as anything Ho himself ever did.

The VNQDD launched its first attack against the French on February 9, 1929, with the assassination of a French official who recruited laborers for the rubber plantations. The assassination took place publicly in Hanoi. But the French authorities struck back quickly, capturing party documents and immediately arresting 229 members of the VNQDD (those arrested reflected the profile of the party: more than 50 percent were in the service of the French administration, almost all had an educated background, and almost all were involved in urban occupations). Curiously, the French did not follow up these arrests with harsh measures, and most of those arrested were soon released. The party was under the leadership of Nguyen Thai Hoc, who, rather than retrenching and working out a better organizational system, decided to strike again, and quickly, to show that the VNQDD was not beaten, but on the contrary, was stronger than ever. He decided to plan mutinies among Vietnamese garrisons in remote outposts. These mutinies were to coincide with demonstrations in Hanoi.

The actual uprising was a disaster. It was delayed because of communications problems, and then, only parts of the network were notified. While most of the conspirators did nothing, two companies of Vietnamese troops revolted in the town of Yen Bay, killing three French officers and two noncoms before they were put down by other, loyal Vietnamese troops. Nguyen Thai Hoc canceled the revolt and fled with twelve of his lieutenants to the Red River delta town of Co An, where they hoped for a peasant uprising. The uprisings were not forthcoming; the local garrisons remained loyal to the French; and the French used air strikes against the town of Co An. It was the first use of air power in Indochina. Though the Vietnamese were showing increasing signs of restlessness, many Frenchmen held on to the idea that they were politically naïve or not interested in politics. Thus at Co An a French journalist reflected in his dispatch some of the new tensions plus the prevailing French viewpoint: "Today I am at Co An and Co An is the most seditious of all communes in Tonkin. If any argument is needed to convince those who believe in the political indifference of the Annamite peasant of their error, I would say that the French authorities judged it necessary to punish an entire village. Co An was bombarded on February 16, 1930, by an air squadron. Five planes . . . after having launched fifty-seven bombs . . . sprayed Co An and the surrounding countryside with machine guns . . ." Soon the thirteen leaders were captured by the French and executed.

The party was in a shambles. It was in even worse shape two years later after the French staged a raid in Hai Duong Province and captured seventy-four members. A few adherents managed to escape to China, and though the VNQDD worked out an arrangement with the Kuomintang a few years later, it was never to be an effective force in Vietnam again. Thus the one non-Communist nationalist group which might have rivaled Ho for power was destroyed. In the late 1940s, when French officials sought a nationalist party as an alternative to Ho and his Communists, they could find no forceful group with any organizational sense or patriotic reputation. The French themselves had seen to that in the early thirties; they had done Ho's work for him and his way now was clearer than ever.

HO WANTED THE GROUP which formed around him in Canton to become committed activists; he made them study Marxism, made two of them join the Chinese Communist party to ensure future contact with it. He sent a third colleague to the Moscow Military Academy so that he in turn might help train future troops of Vietnamese nationalists. Others were sent to China's newly established Whampoa Military Academy, where, under Borodin and Chiang Kai-shek (Chiang was still cooperating with the Communists at the time) and Chou En-lai, the Russians were training the Chinese Army. Ho also dispatched some young men in whom he had great confidence back to Vietnam, where they organized the first cells and staged minor demonstrations against the French. Among these infiltrators was the son of a high-ranking mandarin from the imperial court. He was the brilliant Pham Van Dong, who eventually became Ho's most trusted deputy, and who in intellect and knowledge of his people rivaled Ho himself.

However, the base in Canton was still dependent upon the tenuous relationship between Chiang and the Russians. In 1927 Chiang broke with the Communists and crushed the Canton commune, ruthlessly stamping out many of the Chinese Communists. But Ho and his people, perhaps because as foreigners on Chinese soil they were more sensitive to political nuances—the position of any Vietnamese on Chinese soil was always tenuous—had made contingency plans and most were able to escape, some to Hankow, some to Shanghai and to Hong Kong.

Ho left China, met with the Comintern officials in Moscow, toured Europe and then returned to Asia, this time to Thailand. He worked to organize the sizable Vietnamese community in Bangkok, and helped to create the Comintern's Southeast Asian network. Later he moved into the mountain regions of northern Thailand, founded a Vietnamese paper, and then returned to Bangkok, where, disguised as a Buddhist priest, he studied and preached, teaching the young priests social gospel.

WITH HO IN CANTON and other members in Vietnam, the Thanh Nien group had become badly splintered; it lacked a strong hand to guide it, and events were getting out of control. Unrest had been intensifying inside Vietnam. Part of it was due to greater urbanization and industrialization of the society; there was the beginning of a working class now—a brewery, a rubber plantation, a cement factory. Part of it was the era. The world was simply a more restless, turbulent place. Things which had been impossible before World War I were now suddenly possible. The revolutionary fervor was intensifying. There was a sharp increase in the number of paid workers, from an estimated 12,000 in Tonkin in 1905 to 221,000 by 1929. Similarly the number of strikes began to increase sharply, in part because of natural resentments, and in part because as those resentments developed, the Communists themselves responded to the possibilities and began to provoke more restlessness, thus constantly expanding political activism. In 1928 in all of Vietnam there were only ten strikes with 600 participants; by 1929 there were twenty-four strikes with 6000 participants; by 1930 (with increased Communist political activity now reflected in the figure), there were eighty-three strikes with 27,000 participants. For the Communists this posed something of a problem: were these outbreaks in industry going to give the Vietnamese revolution too openly Marxist (and thus foreign) a character for this basically traditional and rural society? Some of the younger men, feeling that events were outstripping them, felt that the time had come to form a Communist party; the Leninist phase had arrived. Ho wanted no part of this, but he was in Thailand working with the Vietnamese community there (and also working as the Comintern's man in dealing with other Asian countries), and thus unable to control events. He felt a Communist party was premature; he wanted a broader-based nationalist party. When the Thanh Nien party held its congress in Hong Kong in May 1929, the Tonkinese (industrialization was by far the heaviest in their area) demanded the formation of a Communist party. The other delegates seemed to remain loyal to Ho and were against it. Thereupon most of the Tonkinese delegation walked out; they went back and formed their own Indochinese Communist party, shocking the others into the knowledge that things were getting out of control, events were moving faster than they realized. Two other groups now moved ahead, calling themselves Communist parties, one called itself the Indochinese Communist Federation, the other the Vietnamese Communist Party. The exile group from China, now living in Hong Kong, retained the title of Thanh Nien. This deep factionalism of the society would be a constant problem for all Vietnamese political groups; one trusted himself and his family and very few others. Political and secret societies tended to reflect the suspicions of their members and their intellectual arrogance as well. Thus there was a constant problem in trying to expand any political base beyond a specific region or group. (Only Ho's Vietminh would eventually manage to solve this dilemma, aided in no small part by the French decision to fight a war, which gave the Vietminh their great binding cause.) In Moscow the leaders of the Comintern were furious about this divisiveness; the last thing they wanted in an embryonic party was factionalism, with its inevitable consequences—not only would there be a waste of effort and energy, but each faction would betray the other to the French authorities.

Ho, unable to enter Vietnam, was finally dispatched to Hong Kong, where he met with his colleagues, who had slipped into the British territory one by one. The meeting was held in the stands of a soccer stadium, where the roars of the Chinese soccer fans were almost matched by the roars of the Vietnamese politicians. Eventually Ho was able to bring the different factions together under the name Indochinese Communist Party. Shortly afterward he published the party's aims:

1. To overthrow French imperialism, feudalism and the reactionary Vietnamese capitalist class.
2. To make Vietnam completely independent.
3. To establish a government composed of workers, peasants and soldiers.
4. To confiscate the banks and other enterprises belonging to the imperialists and put them under control of the government.
5. To confiscate all of the plantations and property belonging to the imperialists and the Vietnamese reactionary capitalist class, and distribute them to the poor peasants.
6. To implement the eight-hour working day.
7. To abolish public loans and the poll tax. To waive unjust taxes burdening the poor people.
8. To bring back all freedoms to the masses.

9. To carry out universal education.
10. To implement equality between man and woman.

Ho's life was completely clandestine. He changed names and disguises, moving back and forth between Hong Kong and other parts of China and meeting colleagues. "Darling," said a note to another revolutionary, "I await you in Thien Thi's billiard room." Now the fledgling Communist party, seeing the early organizational successes scored by the VNQDD, decided that it must counter with demonstrations of its own, perhaps not so much to overthrow the French as to prevent being outflanked by the non-Communist Nationalists.

So about a year and a half after the early VNQDD uprisings, the Communist leadership started looking for an area where the Communists might be strong and the French weak—unlike the VNQDD, which had struck where the French were strongest. (It was always a mark of the Communists to conserve resources, if at all possible.) They decided on a combined peasants and workers' uprising in the area of Nghe An and Ha Tinh in north-central Vietnam. These were areas where the Communist leadership had particularly strong ties with workers in the towns and their relatives in the villages. The Communists knew that the failure of several harvests had caused growing unrest among the peasants. The leadership of the party decided to go ahead with the uprising, over the opposition of Ho, who was out of the country and thought the demonstration was premature. In February 1930 the first organizers were sent into Nghe An, and starting with May Day 1930 there were incidents and demonstrations for a two-year period. The high point came after the first four months of organizational work during which the Communists, as usual, concentrated on local issues. These preliminaries included protests against high salt prices, demands for destruction of district tax rolls and calls for increased workers' pay. On September 12, 1930, peasants gathered in village after village, formed groups and finally joined in a massive march on Vinh, the provincial capital. When they reached Vinh, more than six thousand demonstrators marched, extending along four kilometers of highway. The French reacted with aircraft, which attacked the column, killing more than two hundred men and wounding another hundred. (More than a year later a French journalist named Andrée Viollis described being outside Vinh and seeing huge tombs along a river bank. Her guide, a French official, told her what they were.

"They date back to September 13 of last year," he told me. "On that morning we suddenly saw an enormous troop of 5000–6000 individuals marching in closed ranks on Vinh . . ."

"Were they armed?"

"Good God, I don't really know. They came supposedly to carry to the Residence their complaints against the taxes, which they considered excessive. This is always the way revolts begin. They were told to stop, but would not listen and crossed the barriers. It was necessary to send planes with bombs against them. About 100 to 120 fell. The others fled like rabbits . . . Unfortunately in the evening, when the people of a village that had remained loyal came to bury the dead, it was thought that this was another demonstration and the planes were sent out again. Result: Another fifteen dead. An awkward error which had a bad effect.")

During this period the Communists also started organizing their own local soviets in village after village in the area. They found that it was not difficult to set them up; village institutions had deteriorated under the French, and both the French and the mandarin governments had proved unresponsive. Though eventually the French made a major pacification effort in the area and destroyed the Communist network, the Communists learned greatly from the experience. The soviets served as a model for some of the cells they formed when they returned to Vietnam a little more than a decade later. In addition, there was considerable reevaluation of successes and mistakes. (This relentless self-criticism would become a Vietminh trademark.) The greatest success had been in using local issues. The most serious error, they decided in retrospect, was the use of terror against lower-echelon Vietnamese exercising authority on behalf of the French, instead of terror aimed at the French themselves. Rather than trying to separate from the French as much of the bourgeoisie as possible, the Indochinese Communist party had driven them to the side of the French. The French were pleased with their success in policing the outbreaks and driving the Communists back into the hills. But there must have been an ominous quality to the experience: the skill of the demonstrators, the organizational strength, the use of peasants as such a disciplined and active political force must have been disquieting. For if the peasants could become a major political force, then the future of France in Indochina was very dubious.

THE FRENCH ADMINISTRATION, sensing first in the Yen Bay revolt and then in the Nghe An strikes that it had, if anything, been too lenient, realizing that its position was becoming hazardous, now struck back hard. Several of Ho's deputies, including Pham Van Dong, were arrested and sent to the dreaded island of Con Son; Tran Phu, the party secretary-general, subsequently died in a Cholon hospital—according to party accounts because he had been brutally tortured. Ho was still in Hong Kong, but the Vinh court sentenced him to death *in absentia,* and the *Sûreté* asked the British authorities to extradite him. The British, worried about unrest in their own Southeast Asian territories, arrested Ho on June 6, 1931, along with two other Comintern agents. The question immediately arose, however, whether the British would turn him over to the French. Two Britons interested themselves in his case: Frank Loseby, a noted anti-imperialist, and Stafford Cripps, who would one day be Chancellor of the Exchequer. They worked tirelessly to prevent Ho's extradition and eventually won their case. Since Ho was a political refugee, he was not subject to extradition.

At this point Ho's health was slipping; he had not been well for several years, apparently suffering from some form of tuberculosis, which had worsened during his stay in the Hong Kong jail. It was typical of his shadowy existence at this time that it was fully recorded that he had died in jail. The French *Sûreté* marked him down as dead; *L'Humanité* and the Soviet press both buried him; Vietnamese students in Moscow held a memorial service for a fallen comrade. (Lacouture notes that little more than a decade later when an alert young French intelligence officer sent a message back to Paris from Cao Bang saying that Ho's name kept cropping up, a high official answered back: "What kind of lunatic is sending us information like that? Everyone knows Nguyen Ai Quoc died in Hong Kong in the early thirties. . . ." Eventually, the *Sûreté* would later identify the real Ho by indentations on his ear lobes.)

Loseby managed to smuggle Ho out of the prison hospital in mid-1932 and slip him aboard a boat going to Fukien Province. He eventually made his way to Shanghai, where he waited for an opportunity to make contact with the Comintern apparatus. He was playing the dangerous game of trying to let the apparatus know who he was without exposing himself to the threat of arrest by Chinese authorities. The Comintern, of course, was particularly suspicious of being involved with someone who had just left a British prison. (Rumors that he worked for the British intelligence service would stay with Ho for more than two decades because of this.)

He did make contact, however, and shortly afterward he slipped back to Moscow, where he attended the Institute for National and Colonial Questions and the well-known graduate school for senior Communist officials, the Lenin Institute. The years that he spent there were turbulent ones in the Communist world; it was the height of the purges: one after another of the great men of the Communist world disappeared as Stalin lashed out again and again. To much of the Caucasian world, Communism would never be viewed in the same way again; the romance of the revolution was now obscured by the new brutality, by the harshness of the one-man dictatorship which was descending.*

But Ho was never harmed by the great Soviet terror. "What is remarkable," wrote Bernard Fall, "is that Ho, as a well-known member of the Comintern group, was not purged right along with them, for hundreds of thousands of people of lesser distinction than he became victims of Stalin's mania. One reason for this may have been his absence from the USSR when the major break came between Stalin and the 'internationalist' wing of the party structure; another may be that Ho, as a doer rather than a theoreti-

* There would never be anything resembling a purge of the Vietnamese Communist leadership; indeed, in 1969 the top group was stunningly similar to what it had been in 1945 at the start of the war. The reason for the stability stemmed from the mutual confidence of Ho and his colleagues. They knew each other, they never doubted each other's legitimacy and commitment. They knew how good they were.

cian, had never participated in the fundamental debates between the Stalinists and their opposition; and lastly, Ho probably was then unconditionally loyal to Stalin and Stalin knew it."

THE PERIOD OF THE POPULAR FRONT, when the Soviet Union decided to cooperate with the Western democracies, was a particularly difficult time for Ho. Nationalist feeling was seething in Vietnam, and now suddenly when it had reached a pitch he had long hoped for, it had to be replaced by a Moscow-based policy of cooperation with the despised French. For Ho himself, the hardened professional revolutionary, Moscow-trained and aware of the importance of Moscow's support, it was a difficult burden but one that he could understand; but for many of the other Vietnamese nationalists it was an outrageous policy. (Indeed, if the VNQDD had not shot its bolt so early in the thirties this might have proved the period in which it could have made great strides against the Communists, for the Communists were tied to international policies, while the VNQDD would have been able to concentrate on local grievances and nationalism.)

Ho left Moscow for Asia. Part of his job was to pacify some of his more restless people who were angry at the limits placed on them during the Popular Front period which began in 1937, a period which saw them moderate their critiques against the French, according to the line laid down by the Soviets. But the Popular Front, with its loosening of the restrictions against indigenous political activity, intensified nationalist ambitions and drives. The Communists were active but wary. Ho himself did not come into Vietnam, and both Giap and Dong operated as part of a front group called the Indochinese Democratic

Front, Dong himself having been arrested in 1931, but released during the amnesty brought on with the Front. In the fall of 1939, the Front abruptly ended, and both Dong and Giap escaped to China, though about two hundred Communists were arrested by the French.

In 1938 Ho had returned to China. Japan was defeating the Chinese in battle after battle, and the threat of Japanese victory brought Chiang and the Communists into another temporary rapprochement. Chiang asked the Communists for guerrilla-warfare instructors, and soon Ho was teaching Chiang's troops. But, more important, he was reunited with Dong, and would meet Giap, the military genius; together the three would make a revolution and form the structure with which to defeat the French.

It had been many years since Ho and Dong had last met, and each was checking out the other's appearance. Ho told another Vietnamese, "Young Dong hasn't aged much," and then, pointing to Giap, said, "He's still as fresh as a girl of twenty." Giap, scheduled by appointment to meet a mysterious Vietnamese sent by the Comintern, wondered whether or not it would be the famed Nguyen Ai Quoc; he sensed it would, and he had carried his picture with him for many years. "A man of mature years stepped towards us, wearing European clothes and a soft felt hat. Compared with the famous photograph, now twenty years old, he looked livelier, more alert. He had let his beard grow. I found myself confronted by a man of shining simplicity. This was the first time I had set eyes on him, yet we were already conscious of deep bonds of friendship . . . He spoke with the accent of central Vietnam. I would never have believed it possible for him to retain the local accent after being abroad for so long . . ."

Yet anyone who knew Ho and his style would have realized that despite his years abroad the things he would be most careful never to lose would be his local accent and his sense of the country and its mores. In fact, when he entered Hanoi in 1945 and addressed his own people for the first time, he said, "I can't tell you what you have to do [to achieve nationhood] but I can show it to you." He put his thumb on the table. "If everywhere you put your thumb on the sacred earth of Vietnam, and a plant will grow, then we will succeed. If not, we will fail." Paul Mus, the French expert on Vietnam, who witnessed the scene, was struck by the fact that this man who had been absent so long had lost no feel or touch for the life of a peasant. "He was on the one hand a Marxist economist who knows the importance of the basic production and on the other hand a Confucian scholar, because what you must keep in mind is the idea that the thumb on the earth is a simple Chinese proverb—a thumb-square of planting rice is more precious than a thumb-square of gold. So you can see how Ho Chi Minh in that situation was directly in contact with the millions of peasants in the rice fields, who at the sight of him were ready to give all their strength, all their devotion to the nation, and if needed, their blood."

NOW WITH WORLD WAR II BREAKING OUT, with the Japanese penetrating farther and farther into Southeast Asia, the possibilities for real revolution mounted. In Europe, Germany marched against France and defeated it; France seemed a rotten core of a nation, as decadent as Ho's speeches had claimed two decades earlier. Thus, Ho knew that the French hold on Vietnam would be weakened, but that it would be replaced by a tougher Japanese hold. He was one of the first to see the possibilities that France would be set back by the Japanese in Asia, that eventually the Allies would defeat Germany and Japan, and that after a war that would be particularly exhausting for the major powers there would probably be a huge vacuum not only in Vietnam but throughout the colonial world. (The great powers, particularly America, were probably not as exhausted as Ho, based on his knowledge of World War I, had imagined they would be.) He further saw that Vietnam would go to the best-organized and best-disciplined indigenous force, which best exploited the war years and devoted its energies to strengthening itself rather than unnecessarily fighting or antagonizing the Japanese or the French. In addition he foresaw a relatively free hand in Asia for the Vietnamese Communist party; the Soviet Union, preoccupied with its own survival, would not be able to issue orders demanding that Ho love the French one month and hate them the next. Thus the Communists could once again be anti-French and no longer worry about a local nationalist party outflanking them.

Ho worked and studied with Dong and Giap in China from 1938 to 1940. Then in the winter of 1940 he set up the first "liberated zone" at Pac Bo in the Cao Bang area, a mountainous region out of reach of the French; for the first time in thirty years he slipped back into his own country.

4

CREATING A NATIONALIST MOVEMENT 1941–1945

*"To be a man, you must endure
the pestle of misfortune."*

HIS ABSENCE had not robbed him of any relevance
or political position; on the contrary, over the years he
had added steadily to his reputation. Now Ho watched
carefully and planned his strategy subtly. In the mountains near the Chinese border he set up headquarters in
a large cave. A nearby peak became Karl Marx Mountain; a stream, Lenin Stream. Day after day he gave in-
struction to his aides. He published a small newspaper,
and now after many years of having to use "Indochinese"
in all titles he could call the paper simply *Viet Lap* (Independent Vietnam).

In early May 1941, far from the world's center stage,
he convened the eighth plenum of the Indochinese Communist party. In a hut, around a bamboo table, the
delegates sat on simple wood blocks. Here a new party
came into being. Its official title was the Vietnam Doc
Lap Dong Minh, or the League for Vietnamese Inde-

pendence—or, for history, the Vietminh. Here, with men who were at once dedicated Communists and ardent nationalists, Ho set the basic policy that would enable this small but brilliantly organized and brilliantly led minority to capture the seething nationalism of Vietnam and make it theirs, to defeat France in one war and to withstand the awesome armed might of America in another. Here Ho told his people that the base of the Vietminh must be as broad as possible, that it must be above all patriotic, that, whatever else, it must be more *Vietnamese* than the opposition—the test of an idea or a policy would be how Vietnamese it was. To form a party that was overtly Communist, he said, would not only alienate potential Vietnamese allies on economic or intellectual grounds, but it might also make the Vietminh vulnerable to the criticism from rival parties that Communists were subject to foreign domination—a damaging charge in a rebellion aimed at evicting a foreign power. So Ho demanded and won a broad National Front which would unite workers, peasants, the petit bourgeois, and even "patriotic landowners."

For more than two decades Ho had been a good international Communist, often swallowing aspects of international Communism which he must have despised, which hurt him politically at home. Now finally he was ideologically free to concentrate on the one idea which had never left his mind: the liberation of his own country. That most powerful force in Vietnam, the longing to get out from under foreign domination, the longing to be Vietnamese again, would become the property of the Vietminh. The flag would be a Vietnamese flag. The Communist party would be a Vietnamese Communist party. The purpose of the struggle would be Cuu Quoc (National Salvation), the program: "After the overthrow of the Japanese fascists and the French imperialists, a revolutionary government of the Democratic Republic of Vietnam will be set up in the new democracy; its emblem will be the red flag with a gold star." In June 1941 Ho crossed over to China briefly and broadcast a famous address which was spread throughout Vietnam, by paper, by word of mouth, in every possible way:

> Now the opportunity has come for our liberation. France itself is unable to dominate our country. As to the Japanese, on the one hand they are bogged down in China, on the other they are hamstrung by the British and American forces and certainly cannot use all of their forces to contend with us. If our entire people are united and single-minded, we can certainly smash the picked French and Japanese armies . . . Several hundreds of years ago when our country was endangered by the Mongolian invasion, our elders under the Tran dynasty rose up indignantly and called on their sons and daughters throughout the country to rise as one in order to kill the enemy . . . Let us unite together! As one in mind and strength we shall overthrow the Japanese and French and their jackals in order to save people from the situation between boiling water and burning heat.

Now he and Giap were no longer just planners. They were activists. Ho translated Chinese and Soviet writings on guerrilla war; Giap trained military cadres and propaganda bands and sent the teams deeper and deeper into Vietnam.

IN 1942 Ho quietly slipped back into China. His most important reason was to work out his relations with Chiang Kai-shek. It was crucial to do this, for it appeared that Chiang might well be the eventual winner in China (he enjoyed reasonably good relations with the Allies), and there was no point in a policy that envisioned the fall of Japan and France but saw Vietnam swallowed up by a hostile Chinese government. A rapprochement was necessary because Ho had been identified with Chiang's domestic enemies. It was at this point that he changed his name for the last time, probably because Nguyen Ai Quoc was a Comintern name and would have antagonized the non-Communist Chinese. He had on some of his Chinese visits used the name Ho Quang and had even been known as Uncle Ho. Now he added the Chi Minh—Ho Who Enlightens.

On this trip he traveled in the guise of a Chinese journalist working in Vietnam, but nonetheless was arrested almost as soon as he crossed over into China. Chiang was not particularly enthused about the prospect of having a Communist government to the South; rather he was interested in seeing the Vietnamese version of his own Kuomintang strengthened. So Ho was arrested and imprisoned.

Once again it was reported that he had died. Giap later recounted: "One day I received a letter from Pham Van Dong . . . informing me that Uncle Ho had just died in the jails of the Kuomintang. We were almost paralyzed with grief. We organized a ceremony of commemoration for our revered leader, and Comrade Dong was given the task of writing his funeral oration. We opened Uncle's rattan case in search of mementos. One of our comrades was dispatched to China with orders to locate his grave . . . A few months later we received a newspaper mailed from China. On the wrapper were a few lines of verse in a hand which was well known to us:

The clouds are setting the peaks aglow
The peaks are hugging the clouds—
I wander alone, roused to feelings,
Scanning the distant southern sky
I am thinking of my friends.

We were wild with joy and no less astonished. We fired question after question at Comrade Dong, who had brought the sad news to us. 'But,' he insisted, 'the Chinese governor told me: "Su Liu! Su Liu! (already dead!)."' 'No, no, your ear confused the tonic accents; what he must have said was "Chu Liu! Chu Liu! (very fit!)."'"

For more than a year Ho was moved from jail to jail while the Chinese tried to influence him to work for them, to head their own Vietnamese nationalist group. It was during this time that he kept his prison notebook, certainly the best writing he ever did: prison thoughts, expressed in poems. The thoughts are simple, edged with a moral tone—a very sharp bite. They reflect his own sense of irony about the injustices he suffered, and yet a complete sense of confidence, as if he knew that being in prison was a required part of his biography, a test to which he was being put, which could only toughen him and prove him more worthy of his people. Indeed, he wrote:

> The rice grain suffers under the pestle;
> yet admire its whiteness when the ordeal is over.
> It is the same with human beings in our time—
> to be a man, you must endure the pestle of misfortune.

Of his chains he wrote in a poem called "The Leg Irons":

> With hungry mouth open like a wicked monster,
> Each night the irons devour the legs of people:
> The jaws grip the right leg of every prisoner:
> Only the left is free to bend and stretch.
>
> Yet there is one thing stranger in this world:
> People rush to place their legs in irons.
> Once they are shackled, they can sleep in peace.
> Otherwise they would have no place to lay their heads.

Or in another called "Autumn Night":

> In front of the gate, the guard stands with his rifle.
> Above, untidy clouds are carrying away the moon.
> The bedbugs are swarming round like army tanks on maneuvers.
> While mosquitoes form squadrons, attacking like fighter planes.
> My heart travels a thousand li toward my native land.
> My dream intertwines with sadness like a skein of a thousand threads.
> Innocent, I have now endured a whole year in prison.
> Using my tears for ink, I turn my thoughts into verses.

And finally:

> . . . Being chained is a luxury to compete for.
> The chained have somewhere to sleep,
> the unchained haven't . . .
> The State treats me to its rice, I lodge in its palaces,
> its guards take turns escorting me.
> Really, the honor is too great . . .

Ho was held in prison for thirteen months. Chiang was in no mood to release him, seeking instead a Vietnamese nationalist group which was at once pro-Chinese and anti-Communist. But just as Chiang's own party was to prove too tied to the past and too feudal in style to survive in the modern age, so did he discover the same problems among his Vietnamese counterparts. He wanted intelligence on the Japanese from them but information was never forthcoming. Frustrated, Chiang decided he needed the Vietminh, after all, but created a new group, the Dong Minh Hoi, in which the Vietminh was just one of ten political groups. By this means he hoped to use the Vietminh intelligence network, which was probably the best in Vietnam, without giving them political control. They of course went along, but failed to send in very much intelligence. Finally, reluctantly, the Chinese decided to release Ho, to make him the head of the Dong Minh Hoi, and to give him what was estimated at $100,000 for his use. It was one more benefit of Ho's truly professional training. One of the lessons Ho had learned, and learned well, from the Russians was the importance of intelligence: place your best men in intelligence, and your even better men in counterintelligence. It was this kind of lesson which Moscow passed on that was particularly valuable for the young party and which allowed them to survive during the clandestine days when other rival parties would prove more vulnerable to the French *deuxième bureau.* Unchained, Ho returned to Vietnam.

IN ONE WAY World War II marked the beginning of the end for the white man in Indochina. The Vietnamese had seen a modern army, but a modern *Asian* one, humiliate the proud Western conqueror. White men who had until recently related to yellow men only as master to serf were now at the mercy of Asians. Thus a rebellion against French authority seemed more than ever a real possibility. It was not ordained forever that white men would rule yellow men. In addition, the strength of the French was limited now: they could no longer control the whole country to the degree they had before; more and more they had pulled back to the larger cities. They were preoccupied with the Japanese, and their hold on the countryside, always considerably weaker than their hold on the cities, was relaxed. Thus the opportunities for infiltration and subversion were greater.

Other nationalist groups were forming too, sensing that the winds were changing and that the old order was on the verge of collapse; the competition among the political groups was heightening. But the other groups tended to be upper-class and better educated; they did not want to change the entire order, just part of it. They wanted to throw off the French but keep their special privilege. Thus—as Ho had realized more than two decades earlier when he opted for Communism—their bourgeois base was likely to be limited. The deep-rooted power it would take to fight the colonialists must be based on more than a parochial sense of injustice. Would enough functionaries, partially blocked in their careers, lay down their lives for a better administrative spot?

(The party which would be the greatest single rival to the Vietminh would be the Dai Viet, but a quick look revealed its weakness in a revolutionary era. It was composed of upper-class Vietnamese—what the Vietminh called "bourgeois nationalists"—men who had gone through the French educational system, receiving the highest degrees. As much as Vietnamese could play a role in colonial life they had played it. They had not worked on expanding their base by indoctrinating peasants, but instead had concentrated on fighting for position and gaining prestige. "The anti-French spirit they manifested," wrote John McAlister, "was emphatically not a result of rejection of French culture, but a result of their impatience at being blocked in their occupational mobility with a French-made framework just short of managing the affairs of their country . . ." The first puppet government which the Japanese formed in April 1945, as the war turned badly, was a largely Dai Viet government of Tran Trong Kim; it included four medical doctors, a professor and a distinguished jurist. These were not the kind of men to lay down their lives readily, nor for whom others would lay down theirs. Their very thin hold on power made the way of the Vietminh easier than might have been expected.)

In addition to being upper-class, these other nationalist groups were often parties or societies of the past. They knew only one thing: they wanted to get the French out. But they lacked the modern skills and structure to enable them to do it. They had not studied under the new professional revolutionaries, who not only dreamed of revolution but spent long hard hours practicing to achieve it: how to put together a party, how to organize a cell, how to keep one cell from knowing of the existence of another (so that a betrayal would have a limited effect), how to pass messages, how to blend military and political propaganda, how to make the military always an arm of the political.

The first lesson of the Vietminh was that the military is useless unless it is totally political, and of course the second lesson was that political skill is useless unless there is comparable military force. Power does flow from the mouth of a gun. Thus by the time World War II was over in 1945, the Vietminh was the one resistance group with a strong military arm.

Much of this professionalism was a reflection of the toughness and skill of Ho. For he was the beaming father figure of his people, the man of constant simplicity, the soft-spoken Asian who seemed gentle, indeed almost sweet, sometimes self-mocking, his humor and warmth in sharp contrast to the normal bureaucratic grimness of a high Communist official. This was the great nationalist who reflected the traditions and aspirations of his people —this was the Gandhi side. But there was the Communist side too. It made him no less a nationalist; indeed he had chosen Communism as the way not because he had any illusions about its harshness, but precisely because he had believed in his youthful desperation that only a force as strong and brutal as Communism could generate the power to make his nationalism succeed. This hard and callous side was rarely seen in public, yet it was always there. He had followed the party line when necessary. He had seen the crimes of Stalin and never flinched. He knew that independence demanded a terrible price, and he was quite prepared to pay it. He was willing to have Giap liquidate rival nationalist elements and willing to turn over to the French *Sûreté* the names of true Vietnamese patriots because they were rivals. It was not that they did not have the same goal as Ho, but that their way to achieve it was different and therefore might endanger Ho's way—which he had decided was the right one. "I am a professional revolutionary. I am always on strict orders. My itinerary is always carefully prescribed —and you can't deviate from the route, can you?" he once told a French Communist friend. He was both the great nationalist and the tough old Bolshevik. (At a funeral service for a Vietnamese nationalist who had been slain because of his Trotskyite views, Ho turned to a friend and said, with great feeling, "He was a great patriot and we mourn him," adding moments later, "All those who do not follow the line which I have laid down will be broken.")

Now as he strengthened the military arm of his party he had the perfect aide, the brilliant, intense Giap, an aristocrat, an educated man with a history degree, who differed from the upper-class mandarins of the Dai Viet in that he had become a full-time revolutionary at an early age; he had forsaken his past while they wanted to hold on to theirs, and to make it fuller. To Western eyes, Giap, who would become one of the great military leaders of the twentieth century, always seemed more militant than Ho, more full of revolutionary fervor, more filled with bitterness against the white man. He had escaped from Vietnam with the end of the Popular Front in 1939, but his wife, also a revolutionary, was captured by the French and died in prison. Giap always believed her death resulted from mistreatment and he became even more passionate a revolutionary. It was Giap who took Ho's ideas and translated them into military terms, who understood how to train and organize troops, and how to exploit the Vietminh's political superiority against the French military superiority. He had needed a military base secure from both the Chinese and the French (and the Japanese too). For this reason he fashioned a wartime friendship with the guerrilla Chu Van Tan, the leader of the Thos, who, unlike most montagnard tribes, were anti-French. The physical impregnability of the base areas of the Thos gave Giap his redoubt. There in December 1944, with two revolvers, seventeen rifles, fourteen flintlock rifles, one light machine gun and thirty-four men, Giap formed the first platoon of the People's Liberation Force.

It was this army that within the next nine years was to grow to six divisions and, as one of the world's great infantry forces, defeat the French at Dienbienphu. There in the mountain hideaway, Giap worked out his essentially simple guerrilla strategy. What did his people have above all else in a showdown with the French? Manpower. What did they lack most? Weapons and materiel. Therefore what should be the heart of the strategy? Go for weapons. Where? Wherever the French were most overextended—in tiny outposts where they were isolated and pinned down, a perfect target, where the Vietminh would know exactly how many Frenchmen with how many weapons were waiting, where no Vietnamese would warn them of the approach of the Vietminh, and finally where the Vietminh could strike in the early morning. If there were ten men inside the post the Vietminh would strike with thirty men. The next day there would be ten more weapons. Then they would hit posts of thirty men. And soon a hundred, and then more. Always striking in superior numbers, always striking where success was almost certain. As Giap's forces grew, he sent them farther into the country to organize villages, to extend the network.

MEANWHILE Ho was sensing the international mood. He knew he had to prepare for war on two fronts. One was the Vietnamese front. With the end of the war coming quickly (because of the atomic bomb it would come even more quickly than he suspected) Vietnam would be in chaos and a vacuum would exist. The group which was best organized, which showed itself to be the most legitimate authority, both to foreigners and to Vietnamese, might gain many long-range benefits by acting quickly.

The second, and closely connected, front was the international one. Here again Ho's remarkable travels would place him far ahead of other Vietnamese leaders in gauging international moves. The French would be weak but would probably try to reassert their authority. The Chinese were a genuinely dangerous force and must not be antagonized (the French were preferable to deal with in some ways, since they were both weaker and logistically farther away). The Americans were a puzzle: they were at once imperialist and anticolonialist, a potential counterforce to the French. So Ho would make himself useful to the Americans. He would help return their downed fliers and speed them useful intelligence about the Japanese. In return they would give him arms. This would be doubly significant. Not only were the arms

73

themselves crucial, but the fact that Vietnamese peasants would know that powerful Westerners were helping Ho would be a great aid in gaining legitimacy. And that was exactly what happened.

The Americans found Ho very helpful and charming indeed. Robert Shaplen has written of the first OSS man who was parachuted into the mountain headquarters. Ho charmed him completely: "He was an awfully sweet old guy. If I had to pick out one quality about that little old man sitting on his hill in the jungle, it was his gentleness," the American recalled. There in the hills the American helped Ho plan raids to free American and French internees, helped him get in touch with French negotiators in Kunming, and helped him frame a Vietnamese declaration of independence. Typically, Ho knew more about the American Declaration than the young American and, just as typically, was deadly serious about it. In August 1945, when the Vietminh seized power, Ho would make a speech to five hundred thousand people gathered in Hanoi. His opening words were: "All men are created equal. They are endowed by their Creator with certain inalienable Rights, among these are Life, Liberty, and the Pursuit of Happiness . . ." Ho also kept up a surprisingly grammatical correspondence with the young American:

Dear Lt. I feel weaker since you left. Maybe I'd have to follow your advice—moving to some other place where food is easy to get to improve my health . . .
I'm sending you a bottle of wine, hope you like it.
Be so kind as to give me foreign news you got . . .
Please be good enuf to send to your H.Q. the following wires:
National Liberation Committee of VML begs U.S.A. authorities to inform United Nations the following. We were fighting Japs on the side of the United Nations. Now Japs surrendered. We beg United Nations to realize their

solemn promise that all nationalities will be given democracy and independence. If United Nations forget their
solemn promise and don't grant Indo-China full independence, we will keep on fighting until we get it.

Signed—National Liberation Committee of VML.

Thank you for all troubles I give you . . . best greetings.

Yours sincerely,

Hoo [sic]

In early 1945 Ho apparently visited Kunming, where
he presented his case for weapons to the American mission
there. The American in charge laid down strict conditions:
that the weapons not be used against the French, and
that American agents be permitted into the rebel-con-
trolled areas. The Americans later claimed that they gave
Ho only a few revolvers, although there is considerable
evidence that five thousand weapons were airdropped to
the Vietminh in the summer of 1945 by the Allies. Also
according to both French and Communist accounts, the
number of Vietminh troops in the country at the time
of the fall of Japan, was five thousand. Five thousand
weapons may not have been many by Western standards,
but it was far more than any other resistance group had.
The Vietminh's sense of weaponry made its organization
seem much more impressive—the number of weapons
multiplied in the minds of the population and the opposition (indeed, one handmade weapon could control a
village in the early days of the war). Steadily Giap infiltrated his troops farther into the country; by June 1945
he controlled six provinces in northern Vietnam, and he
was extending that control all the time; more important,
Giap's was the only nonforeign military force.

THE COLLAPSE OF THE JAPANESE came very suddenly. Of all the Vietnamese groups, only one was ready

with a scenario for the occasion. Only one knew how to organize shock troops, how to stir public demonstrations and then turn the public mood to its own favor. That was the Vietminh. In August 1945 they moved into the vacuum and seized power with what in retrospect seems almost ridiculous ease.

On August 17, immediately after the Japanese surrender, a coalition group of Emperor Bao Dai, regarded by most Vietnamese as a puppet figure, and the Dai Viet, the largely upper-class party, held a mass meeting in Hanoi. It turned out to be a massive mistake, since the strength of this group was more in bureaucratic control than in revolutionary fervor and public demonstration. More than 150,000 people showed up. It was a crucial moment. Suddenly at the height of the meeting, Vietminh flags appeared everywhere. One was on the rostrum. The people started cheering. A Vietminh speaker attacked the Tran Trong Kim group as weak, and proclaimed that only a truly revolutionary group was strong enough to wrest power from the Japanese and French. The speaker demanded: "Let us unite together in a single bloc. The independence of the Fatherland can be won only by blood . . . We must take arms and rise up." It was a stirring appeal at a time when public enthusiasm and militancy ran strong. The Vietminh leaders then turned the demonstration into a street parade through Hanoi, showing Vietminh propaganda banners and the Vietminh flag. Before the demonstration was over, about a hundred local-government militia men had joined the parade. It was an exciting time for all Vietnamese: the war had ended, the white man's grip seemed to be weakening before their eyes, and here was the Vietminh promising a revolution—and leading it. Similar scenes were taking place in Saigon and Hué. The Vietminh had organized the cities, they had seized the initiative, seized the very excitement and drama of the occasion itself and made it theirs.

The student groups had been growing more and more powerful in the occupation years. One reason was that the French, fearing that their influence might ebb during the Japanese occupation, had instituted a massive sports and physical-education program, which turned out to be an ideal leadership-training ground for Vietnamese nationalism. Students were now faced with a choice between the leadership of the tired old upper class that held its mandate from the Japanese or the Vietminh, legendary folk heroes who had always fought the colonialists and who now stepped out of their mountain hideouts and walked into Hanoi as liberators. The decision was inevitable. Within hours the students became a vital part of the Vietminh shock machinery.

By August 19, having succeeded with political tactics, the Vietminh was ready to show its military hand as well. On that morning about a thousand armed Vietminh troops walked into Hanoi and seized control. Somehow there seemed to be more of them than there actually were. The Japanese-installed government was caught by surprise. The 30,000 Japanese troops offered no resistance. The local Hanoi police and militia wavered at first. But soon they became caught up in the rising tide of the day, for they saw the force of the Vietminh in action: these soldiers seemed to know what they were doing; they seemed to be already in charge. Sensing the need for a symbolic gesture, the Vietminh stormed the official residence of the imperial delegate, only to find that he had fled the city. To anyone who knew what had happened during the Soviet takeover in Eastern Europe the pattern was familiar: neutralization of the local armed units, takeover

77

of the key administrative offices and the public utilities. All was organized, and all was easy. The city was filled with revolutionary excitement.

Even Bao Dai prophetically cabled De Gaulle telling him not to send French troops to Vietnam: "You could understand even better if you were able to see what is happening here, if you were able to sense the desire for independence that has been smoldering in the bottom of all hearts, and which no human force can any longer hold back. Even if you were to arrive to reestablish a French administration here, it would no longer be obeyed; each village would be a nest of resistance, every former friend an enemy, and your officials and colonials themselves would ask to depart from this unbreathable atmosphere."

On August 22 Bao Dai, sensing the inevitable, asked the Vietminh to form a government. The Vietminh, wary that Bao Dai might turn out to be a rival for legitimacy, demanded that he withdraw. On August 25, Bao Dai abdicated and accepted, under the name of citizen Vinh Thuy, the title Supreme Political Adviser. The Vietminh were still seeking the broadest possible base.

Now, finally, the way was set.

5

PATH TO DIENBIENPHU: THE TIGER DEFEATS THE ELEPHANT 1945–1954

"We will be like the elephant and the tiger. When the elephant is strong and rested and near his base we will retreat. And if the tiger ever pauses, the elephant will impale him on his mighty tusks. But the tiger will not pause and the elephant will die of exhaustion and loss of blood."

FOR THE FIRST FEW DAYS Ho stayed out of Hanoi. The powerful, tightly organized operation which he had conceived up in the mountains had worked very well under the careful and ruthless eye of Giap; there was no need for Ho to lead the parade into Hanoi. In addition he and Giap remained suspicious of the Japanese. What game were they playing? Might they use this neutral tactic as a means of flushing Ho out, then grab him and use him as a pawn in subsequent negotiations with the French?

Ho quietly entered the city around August 25, but still did not surface. Meanwhile, organizational meetings were taking place throughout Hanoi as the Vietminh incorporated other groups into their structure. A student named Nguyen Manh Ha, leader of a Catholic student group, was appointed the first Minister of National Economy under the Vietminh. He recalled that there was much discussion during those first exciting days about the actual identity of the Vietminh leader. Some said he was Ho Chi Minh. Some said he was the famed Nguyen Ai Quoc. Some said Ho Chi Minh *was* Nguyen Ai Quoc, "the revolutionary whose name had haunted and fired our imaginations when we were young." On the night of the twenty-fifth, Giap finally told Nguyen Manh Ha and his colleagues that Ho would be present the next day. Ha recalled: "The next day as we stood chatting in the corridors we saw a strange-looking figure coming toward us, clad in shorts, carrying a walking stick and wearing a most peculiar brown-painted colonial helmet. He looked like a real character. Who was he? A rural *can bo* [cadre] fresh from the paddies? A scholar from some outlying part? But our attention was caught by a detail which in those days was altogether unusual and which made it obvious that here was no ordinary party member—a packet of American cigarettes was sticking out of his shirt pocket . . ." Later, Ha observed: "He was very easygoing at cabinet meetings. On September 1, the eve of the declaration of independence, he arrived with a scrap of paper on which he had drafted his proclamation to the people. He submitted it to us, passing it around, accepting amendments—though at this stage, before the anti-Communist nationalists came into the government, there was little that needed debating within the cabinet . . ."

On August 30 the Vietminh announced the Cabinet. The President would be Ho Chi Minh. Ho Chi Minh?—a name still barely known to most Vietnamese. Some maintained he was the famous Nguyen Ai Quoc.* Asked about

---

* He remained for some years sensitive about the dual identity of Ho Chi Minh and Nguyen Ai Quoc. In 1946, during talks with General Salan, the French officer in charge of truce negotiations, Salan asked him

his identity by journalists in Hanoi at the time, Ho answered, with vintage cult-of-simplicity: "I am a revolutionary. I was born at a time when my country was already a slave state. From the days of my youth I have fought to free it. That is my one merit. In consideration of my past, my companions have voted me head of government." It was an extraordinary answer, as if he were saying, "My name is not important, but I am your sorrows, your being imprisoned by the whites; I am the embodiment of your revolution. I am more than your father; I am your spirit."

On September 2, Ho made his declaration of independence speech, blending the American Declaration of Independence with the French Declaration of the Rights of Man. The French, he said, had systematically violated those rights in Vietnam. Then he said that the Vietminh, representing the downtrodden Vietnamese people, had seized power, not from the French but from the Japanese. "Since the autumn of 1940 our country has ceased to be a colony and had become a Japanese outpost . . . We have wrested our independence from the Japanese and not from the French. The French have fled, the Japanese have capitulated, Emperor Bao Dai has abdicated, our people have broken down the fetters which for over a century have tied us down; our people have at the same time overthrown the monarchic constitution that had reigned supreme for so many centuries and instead have established the present Republican government."

---

point-blank if he was Nguyen Ai Quoc. Ho categorically denied it. Similarly in 1946 when Vo Quy Huan, a technician whom Ho had brought back from Paris to work with him, asked where Nguyen Ai Quoc was at the moment, Ho answered, "You'd better ask him, not me." By 1958, however, official Hanoi publications admitted that Ho and Nguyen were the same man.

THUS WITHIN TEN DAYS after the fall of the Japanese, the Vietminh controlled Vietnam, and Ho was President. Independence, of course, would not come all at once. No one knew better than he that the hold was a shaky one, that the Japanese must be dealt with, that the French would almost surely try to reassert their authority. And yet no one knew better than he what a crucial coup he had accomplished. It was almost incredible to him. He had sat there in the mountains and talked of it—the decay of the French, the pull-out of the Japanese, the weakness of the other nationalist groups—but to plan and to accomplish were quite different. Ho had written the scenario and miraculously everyone had played his part perfectly. Now, of course, there would be problems— perhaps even a war; perhaps much blood spilled and much bitterness and pain, but that was almost secondary, for Ho realized what few others did: that it would all derive from August 1945. For it was then that the Vietminh had in one quick stroke taken over the nationalism of the country, that Ho had achieved the legitimacy of power. When the French dealt with the Vietnamese from now on, they would have to deal with him. When they challenged him now they would only increase his authority; when they fought him in battle they would strengthen him more—the French would do his work for him. He had established legitimacy over the other groups, had become the arbiter of Vietnamese nationalism. Though it was not inevitable that he would succeed immediately and easily, he was sure that if it became a question of a long, drawn-out war, the French would have to give first. He felt that history was on his side for the first time.

Ho was President now, but his age showed. Harold

Isaacs, an American journalist with deep sympathy for Vietnamese nationalism, had known Ho in Shanghai in 1933. Now Isaacs barely recognized his old friend. Ho had aged immensely, Isaacs thought, in the twelve years —had become an old man, his hair gray, his cheeks hollow, "his skin like old paper," many of his teeth missing. Isaacs was a man to be trusted because he had been friendly to a powerless Asian exile, and so Ho talked at length with him, telling of his travels, right through to the Chinese prisons. "All the way up to Liuchow and Kweilin," he grinned. "It was at Kweilin that my teeth began to fall out. I looked at myself once and then tried never to look again. I was skin on bones and covered with rotten sores. I guess I was pretty sick." That night he took Isaacs to dinner: "Come on, you will have dinner with the President of the Republic." They went through a corridor and two young Vietminh guards snapped to attention and, their revolvers showing, followed Ho to his car. Ho laughed. "How funny life is! When I was in prison in China I was let out for fifteen minutes in the morning and fifteen minutes in the evening for exercise. And while I took my exercise in the yard, there were always two armed guards standing right over me with their guns. Now I'm President of the Vietnam Republic, and whenever I leave this place there are two armed guards right over me, with their guns."

Ho was aware that he had moved swiftly, at a time when the French were still staggering under their own defeats, but that sooner or later they would have to be contended with, as would the Chinese. Eventually he would have to make some accommodations to one of the two powers. To his mind, France, distant and now weak, was preferable to a China which shared a common border and had a traditional taste for southward expansion. "It is better to sniff the French dung for a while than to eat China's all our lives," Ho told a friend at the time. It would not be easy to deal with France without cooling the passion of his own people, without seeming like a lackey. Annoyed by the virulent anti-French propaganda of Tran Huy Lieu, the Minister of Propaganda, Ho once lost his temper at a cabinet meeting and said: "All right, so it's fun abusing the colonialists. And where does it get you?" He would be dealing with the French from a position of limited strength; they had a military potential he lacked.

The French, of course, had their own problems. Though they were sure they could overwhelm the Vietminh, there were the military and economic considerations of a long war. (Leclerc, De Gaulle's man there, well advised by the distinguished scholar Paul Mus, sensed immediately the guerrilla possibilities for the Vietminh if they chose to fight a rural-based war: "It would take 500,000 men to do it, and even then it could not be done," he told Mus even before the start of hostilities.) Could France, not yet recovered from its disastrous experience in World War II, absorb this struggle without paying a prohibitive price itself? Negotiations began. Ho had made his position clear to Paul Mus: "I have no Army. I have no finance. I have no diplomacy. I have no public schools. I have just hatred and I will not disarm it until you give me confidence in you." The French representative was Jean Sainteny, and the Vietnamese was Ho. Each had his more militant colleagues. The negotiations were long and difficult. The main problem was the question of how much freedom there would be for the Vietnamese, and what the outlines of French sovereignty would be. The Vietminh had proclaimed *doc lap* on September 2. Now there was disagreement between Ho and the French as to its exact meaning. Did it mean freedom, as some claimed, or did it mean independence, as Ho and his colleagues claimed? And what was the exact distinction between the two?

During those early weeks of negotiation, Ho seemed more anxious than the others for some kind of rapprochement with the French. Perhaps it was because he saw a genuine chance to blend the two cultures, and to use French technology to speed Vietnam into the modern world; perhaps because he saw that the alternative was a long and particularly brutal war, and thought that a few years in a semi-independent union was preferable. Whenever he saw newspapermen he went out of his way to emphasize common ties with France: "France and Vietnam were married a long time ago. The marriage has not always been a happy one, but we have nothing to gain from breaking it up . . . France is a strange country. It is a breeding ground of admirable ideas, but when it travels it does not export them. . . ." Sainteny, who was to retain respect and admiration for Ho, would later write that Ho seemed genuinely repelled by the idea of solving the conflict by arms. "There is no doubt that he had aspirations throughout this period of becoming the Gandhi of Indochina."

And yet negotiations were still going badly. In March 1946, with a French convoy sailing toward Hanoi, the tension mounted; the difference between the two sides seemed insurmountable. Most journalists believed war was about to start. On the last day before the convoy arrived, Ho and Sainteny worked far into the night. Ho seemed to be giving way on *doc lap* and on a relationship with the French Union, but there was sharp disagreement on the status of Cochin China. Finally, very early in the morning, Ho called Sainteny and accepted his terms; the next day, March 6, just when war might have broken out, an agreement was signed.

The Vietminh seemed to have given more than the French. The French recognized the government of Vietnam as a free state with its own government, parliament and finances, forming part of the Indochinese federation and the French Union. But the Vietnamese pledged to give a friendly welcome to French military forces as they relieved the Chinese and remaining Japanese—that was the painful part. The two sides agreed that frank negotiations should open between them to work out the exact details. Sainteny then told Ho how pleased he was with the agreement. "I'm not so pleased," Ho answered, "for really it is you who have benefited; you know perfectly well I wanted more than this . . . Still, one can't have everything overnight."

The immediate reaction among the Vietnamese population was very negative. Ho was accused of being a spy, a French agent, a betrayer. Long accustomed to seeing their representatives exploit their positions for selfish advantage, the Vietnamese people were supersensitive to betrayal—they smelled it before it existed. They always expected the worst, and usually were not disappointed. That night the Vietminh officials went before an enormous audience to explain the accords. The crowd was angry and sullen. Even when Giap spoke and said that the accords had been signed as a means of buying time, comparing it to the Soviet Union's signing the Treaty of Brest-Litovsk in 1918 in order to halt the German invasion, the crowd remained mutinous. Then Ho spoke.

There were tears in his eyes as he explained his decision: he had negotiated rather than lose fifty or a hundred thousand lives; he hoped that total freedom would come in five years. He ended: "I, Ho Chi Minh have always led you along the path to freedom; I have spent my whole life fighting for our country's independence. You know I would sooner die than betray the nation. I swear I have not betrayed you." There and then he won a roaring acceptance of the accords from his own people.

BUT FORCES ON BOTH SIDES would make this agreement tenuous; its strength, indeed its life, stemmed from its vagueness. In subsequent months, as Ho and others tried to work out further details, the French reaction would begin to harden. Admiral d'Argenlieu, the Governor General of Indochina, a man still seeking France's manifest imperial destiny, told Leclerc's deputy: "I am amazed, yes, General, that is the word, I am amazed that France has in Indochina such a fine expeditionary force, and that its chiefs prefer to negotiate rather than to fight." He followed up by trying to subvert the agreements in every way—and it was not hard. Soon after the signing of the accords, danger signals began to sound on both sides. In May 1946, Ho left for France to negotiate the final treaty. The outcome was to be disastrous.

France was a defeated and uncertain nation: it had left colonial matters to "the specialists," that is, the right-wing ultraconservatives in the Ministry of Colonies who reflected the old order's pride and prejudices, and the special interests of the great colonial firms.

Most of the colons were with Admiral d'Argenlieu; they saw the Vietnamese as they had always wanted to see them—docile, loving, grateful for the French experience. (When the war broke out and the Vietminh struck, "the old Indochina hands were indignant." Lucien Bodard quoted them: " 'Sir, if we had had the sense to cut off a few dozen heads at the right moment there would still be a French Indochina. After all before 1940 absolutely any Frenchman could travel wherever he liked, even in the wildest districts without carrying a weapon. The village notables were only too happy to welcome him with deep bows.' The speakers were men of standing, respectable, worthy, jovial citizens with fat little bellies—the old 'colonial egg'—on spindly legs. They described the old Indochina, the Indochina of sixty years' Protectorate, as an earthly Paradise. 'What didn't we do for the *nha ques?*' they said to me. 'We rescued them from abject poverty, we gave them schools, roads and hospitals; and what is even more important, we brought them justice and security. But how can a country so overwhelmed with kindness possibly have blown up in our faces like this? Did not these happy people really want independence more than anything else . . . If they [Paris] had only listened to us! We who understood the Annamese so well—we who loved them and were loved in return. But these people accused us of exploiting the Annamese: indeed they very nearly took their side against us.' ")

Thus the French government was not showing the face the Vietnamese might have expected to see—nor even the one it expected to show. Ho, for his part, apparently overestimated the support and influence he would receive from his old friends in the French Socialist and Communist parties.

In France Ho charmed all. Reporters who visited him found him engaging, witty, self-mocking. Women came and were given flowers. But the strain between Ho and his hosts was great. The French had given him a giant red carpet at his hotel when he first arrived, as was customary for a visiting chief of state. But David Ben Gurion, who happened to be in Paris, noticed that "Ho's descending fortunes could be measured by the progressive shrinking of the protocolary carpet. On Ho's arrival it had extended from the sidewalk to his room. As the summer wore on, it was limited to the lobby, then to the staircase, and finally simply to the corridor in front of Ho's suite."

The old problems still remained unchanged: The Vietnamese wanted independence and a weak form of association with the French. The French wanted guided self-government within the French Union, with France controlling the sovereignty of Vietnam (this would mean a French hold on the crucial ministries). Days and weeks passed, and the gap between Ho and the French never seemed to narrow.

In Paris Ho was interviewed by the distinguished American journalist David Schoenbrun. "If the French do not give you some form of independence, President Ho, what will you do?" asked Schoenbrun.

"Why, we will fight, of course," said Ho.

"But, President Ho," continued Schoenbrun, "the French are a powerful nation. They have airplanes and tanks and modern weapons. You have no modern weapons, no airplanes, no tanks. Not even uniforms. You are peasants. How can you fight them?"

"We will be like the elephant and the tiger. When the elephant is strong and rested and near his base we will retreat. And if the tiger ever pauses, the elephant will impale him on his mighty tusks. But the tiger will not pause and the elephant will die of exhaustion and loss of blood," Ho said.*

* Ho's prophecy was strikingly like that of Marshall Tran Hung Dao, who, when the Mongols invaded Vietnam for the third time in 1284, wrote: "The enemy must fight his battles far from his home base for a long time. We must further weaken him by drawing him into protracted campaigns. Once his initial dash is broken, it will be easier to destroy him." In that campaign, the Vietnamese wore the Mongols

89

Yet the French did not take the Vietnamese determination seriously. The negotiations still did not go well. To the French, a war was unthinkable; but the alternative, giving away independence to little yellow men who could be so easily dominated, was even more unthinkable. If *les jaunes* were to get independence (if they were "ready" for it—that was the phrase in those days) then it would be in good time, when the French decided to grant it through largesse—but it would not be extorted at gunpoint. It would take Ho and Giap eight bitter years of war to prove that this thinking was poor morality, poor politics and indeed poor military logic—and it would be a painful lesson for France in the learning. (Indeed in 1954 few would doubt that the Vietnamese were ready for independence.) But in 1946 the French establishment was interested in what it considered to be the restoration of France's greatness. (Britain, which had come out of the great war with its national pride more intact, was able to handle the loss of its great jewel, India, with far greater skill than that with which the humiliated French would handle the question of Vietnam.) At the negotiations, the French were unyielding. Ho pleaded with the French about the toughness of the terms: "Don't leave me this way; arm me against those who seek to surpass me. You will not regret it." It was a typical performance for Ho, in that he was at once trying to show himself as more

down with a grinding, painful, frustrating war. When the Mongols were finally ready to withdraw, Tran Hung Dao planted thousands of iron-tipped stakes in the Bach-Dong River north of Haiphong, through which the Mongol fleet had to pass. The ships arrived at high tide when the stakes were submerged; a small Vietnamese naval force decoyed the enemy into a fight and what looked like an easy Mongol victory, until suddenly the Mongol ships found themselves stranded or gored on the stakes. At that point the Vietnamese infantry charged and destroyed the invaders. It was the type of battle which, in only slightly different form, the French would see a great deal of in future years: the exploitation of terrain, the deception, the ambush.

reasonable than the others on his side, such as Giap—and all the while he was buying time for Giap. The French did not arm him against his own; there was no softening of the line. On September 14, 1946, in an eleventh-hour decision not unlike the earlier one—always buying time? always Brest-Litovsk?—Ho finally signed a modus vivendi.

It was in effect an agreement to disagree, a decision which solved nothing and which only meant that the anti-negotiation forces on both sides would become stronger in the coming months. His red carpet gone, Ho left Paris, sure that war was coming. He had not wanted war; even those who, like Sainteny, had negotiated with him thought he sincerely wanted peace. But it had been too much to ask the French to grant independence; finally one must fight for it.

At home, during the Paris negotiations, Giap had been using his tough, brilliant organizational techniques to quietly wipe out some rival nationalists. He had also expanded the Vietminh structure village by village to a degree that surprised even his colleagues. (At the outbreak of hostilities there would be well more than 100,000 Vietminh under arms. Equally important, more than 75,000 of them would be north of the Seventeenth Parallel, where, under the existing agreements, the French had only 15,000 men.) If there were to be a war, then this was the time—while the French military presence was still slight.

On December 18, 1946, the Vietminh struck and the Indochina war was on.

IT WAS A REVOLUTIONARY WAR, that is, it was at once warfare and revolution. It was brilliantly conceived and brilliantly executed. Political considerations were always of the essence. The Vietminh leaders considered that reaching the mind of the guerrilla was their most important object. He must know who he was fighting and why, as must the simple peasants around him. Even as the war continued it seemed to strengthen the Vietminh politically at home. The French did his recruiting for him. Each day the war went on, the job for Ho and Giap became easier—less the minority Communist party against the French nation, and more the Vietnamese nation against the colonial oppressor. His opponents thus were being swept aside: to be Ho's political opponent now was to be an enemy of the Vietnamese people.

The French and the rest of the Western world read the daily dispatches telling of the noble struggle of the West against the Communists, and noted approvingly what seemed to be an endless stream of French victories. But for the Vietnamese it was another war; it was the struggle not for Communism, but to throw the white colonialist out. The most restless and patriotic men of a generation signed up with the Vietminh, for *this* was the great cause. This was the heroic war for freedom. All those long-submerged and powerful Vietnamese aspirations were unleashed—and the Vietminh harnessed them to their revolution.

The Vietminh were always sensitive to local nuance, always sensitive to Vietnamese tradition. A captured soldier was once asked by interrogators: "When you joined the Front did you tell your family?" This, after all, was the critical question; the greatest loyalty is to the family. "No, I did not," he said, "I felt it was my filial duty, but I talked to the Front and they said to me, 'Comrade, your words show that you are a fine son filled with filial piety and we admire that very much, but in the face of the loss and destruction of your country you have to choose between filial duty and duty toward your country. In this war the people are your family too, and you have to suffer. If you do your duty toward your parents—tell them of your decision—then you fail your country. But if you fulfill your duty toward your country, then by the same act you will have completed your duty toward your family, because they will be free and no longer exploited.' "

For a Vietnamese of that generation there was only one question: Which side are you on, the Vietnamese side or the colonialist side? And from this passion, the Vietminh over a period of eight years welded an extraordinary political and military force. To the peasant, consigned by birth to a life of misery, poverty, ignorance, the Vietminh showed a way out. A man could be as good as his innate talent permitted; lack of privilege was for the first time in centuries not a handicap—if anything, it was an asset.*
One could fight and die serving the nation, liberating both the nation and oneself. Nepotism and privilege, which had dominated the feudal society of the past, were wiped away. One rose only by ability. (After all, the French had all the air power: could you really put a brother-in-law in charge of a battalion when one false step, one mistake in camouflage, could mean that the battalion was wiped out?) And in putting all this extraordinary human machinery together, the Vietminh gave a sense of nation to this formerly suspicious and fragmented society, until at last that which united the Vietnamese was more power-

---

* I remember in 1967 interviewing a Vietminh colonel who had defected to the American side. He had been one of the earliest members of the Vietminh, had risen high, had commanded a battalion. But his father, he said, had been something of an itinerant medicine man. Although the son had joined as early as 1945, he spoke with a slightly better accent and dressed a little better than the other soldiers, and he was sure that even though he had excelled in combat, his lack of true peasant origins had been held against him. Perhaps, he said, "If I had been born a peasant, I would be a general now . . ."

ful than that which divided them—until they were in fact a nation, just as Ho had claimed. (This would contrast sharply with the world of French- and American-sponsored Saigon, where even in 1969, when the fear of the city's falling into Communist hands loomed large, that which divided the South Vietnamese leadership was still more powerful than that which united them. The old petty jealousies remained; it was still a feudal society.)

The French never really understood the war; as the Americans would, they thought of it in terms of terrain controlled, bodies counted; they heard of supply problems and shortages among the Vietminh and were sure that collapse was imminent. From time to time they met with Vietminh units face to face, and on those occasions killed more of the enemy than they lost themselves. This they would claim as a victory. It would be extensively reported in the French press. They never considered that perhaps the battle had taken place precisely because the Vietminh had wanted it, that despite the apparent imbalance in casualties, the Vietminh might well be the winner because the Vietnamese people would find the greater casualties somehow more bearable than would the French people thousands of miles away. For to the French it was a distant war, a war of vanity and pride, whereas to the Vietnamese it was a war of survival; they would pay any price. "It is the duty of my generation to die for our country," one Vietminh soldier told an American at the time. The casualty lists might be heavy but they were acceptable—anything as precious as independence could not come cheap.

The French never understood that the fact that they had absolute military superiority was illusory because the Vietminh had absolute political superiority. And since this was a political war, it meant that in the long run the Vietminh had the absolute superiority. The French, like the

Americans after them, would fight limited war against a smaller nation that, in contrast, fought *total* war, a war of survival. For time was on the Vietminh side. Though the French might win a single battle, battles meant nothing; it was not a war for control of land, but for control of people and their minds, and here the Vietminh was unchallenged. Indeed, the very victories of the French came back to haunt them—there would inevitably be dead civilians left behind, and their relatives would see the corpses. That night Vietminh agents would slip into the village, and sign more recruits.

Even the white skin of the French troops was a symbol of their alien role. Enemies seemed everywhere. Every Vietnamese servant, houseboy or clerk was a potential Vietminh agent; every woman in every village, a potential spy, telling the Vietminh exactly where a French patrol had gone, how many men were in it, what kind of weapons they carried, but telling the French nothing. The ambush was the key to Vietminh tactics; it was perfectly designed for their kind of war. Aided by the warnings of the population, the Viets could blend into the scenery the way the French could not. The very fear of an ambush eventually became a deterrent, making the French wary of going into the interior. This allowed the Vietminh more time to propagandize, to recruit among the population. Again and again it would happen: the French convoy moving slowly, ponderously ahead, watching for mines, when suddenly thousands of Vietminh would attack. It was, said one young French officer recounting a typical ambush, "an execution."

For a few minutes the column fought back furiously, weaving to and fro and breaking into thousands of separate personal battles . . . But there were too many Viets; the ones who were killed didn't count—there were always

95

more, coming from behind every bush and every rock. Each of us had to go through those appalling seconds when you feel there is no possibility of resistance any more and that now you are merely something to be killed off. And with some of us this was mixed up with a realization of an impossible state of affairs—that Europeans could be wiped out in this way by Asians. But the column was already in its death throes. There was a silence over the destroyed column: and a smell. That silence, you know, with the groaning in it; and that smell . . . of bodies which comes when there has been a great slaughter—they are the first realities of defeat. Then presently there was another reality, and a far more surprising one—that of the Vietminh discipline. I had expected barbarity; but within a few moments after the last shot what I saw was an extraordinary scrupulousness—the establishment of exact order. Viet officers moved about the battlefield, but not at all as conquerors— merely as though one operation had been finished and another was beginning. I could not make out any vanity in them—no triumph. They looked into everything, they took notes, they gave orders to their men. . . . Elsewhere soldiers with submachine guns herded the prisoners together, formed them up and led them off. It was all done without savagery, without brutality, and without pity either, as though everything that had to do with humanity or inhumanity did not count; as though one were in a world with new values. I was face to face with the ethics of the Communist order; it was something of an absolute nature, a thousand times beyond anything we call discipline. Instead of knocking everybody on the head from now on, the Viets were caring for the wounded and taking prisoners; for they had learned a new technique from the Chinese for dealing with men, an infallible, irresistible technique that worked even better when it was applied to the worst, most atrocious enemies, including colonialists. This was reeducation. . . ."

The Vietminh could be everywhere and nowhere; they did not have to be in a village to control it. They found it easy to introduce an excellent, completely indigenous political organization to run the village and keep it in line. Such an organization intimidated any possibly pro-French elements. Often these sympathizers were publicly assassinated—a symbol of what might happen to friends of the colonialist, a reminder that the French could not protect their own. The French were weak in the villages; they had to be there physically to dominate them. In order to control terrain, the French had to stand on it, and the terrain absorbed them, sucked them down; it was a quagmire, first to the French and then to the Americans. Five hundred thousand men sounded like a lot, but they would be tied to fixed points, bogged down, the Vietminh always knowing exactly where they were, they never knowing where the Vietminh were, the Vietminh shifting, regrouping. The terrain was the friend of the Vietminh. They could do very few things, but they did them well: the ambush, camouflage, and finally the assault. To the French the jungle was an enemy, the night was an enemy; danger was everywhere. To the Vietminh the night and the jungle were friends, offering protection against airplanes and tanks. And they taught this to the peasants, destroying his fear of the night and the jungle.

And always the revolution went on—the indoctrination against the French and the wealthy class, and the dividing up of land which they had taken. The Vietminh took the young peasants who had been beaten down by the system and told them that they were as good as the French and the mandarins, that they were as strong and as talented as the upper class, and that, yes, they could rise up. Above all the Vietminh gave the peasant a sense of being a person. Those who had been shown again and again their lack of value now found that they had their rights too—even if only the right to die for an idea, that smallest right. And in doing this the Vietminh finally produced an extraordinary revolutionary force, whose bravery was stunning, which believed in itself and its cause.

The Vietminh leadership understood exactly both its own strengths and limitations, and using its strengths, it created a new form of modern revolutionary warfare—political, psychological, and of course military. The Vietminh had decided regretfully that human life was a small price to pay for freedom. Yes, use terror, but use it discriminately. Terrorize the right person, one already despised in the village, showing the villagers that you have the capacity to strike audaciously, and that you are on their side against the hated officials. Whatever grievances existed against the old order, and there were many, the Vietminh took over and exploited politically.

In Graham Greene's *The Quiet American*, when Pyle, the young CIA agent, talks about the Communists' destroying the freedom of the individual, the sour British narrator answers: "But who cared about the individuality of the man in the paddyfield? . . . The only man to treat him as man is the political commissar. He'll sit in his hut and ask his name and listen to his complaints; he'll give up an hour a day to teach him—it doesn't matter what, he's being treated like a man, like someone of value. Don't go on in the East with that parrot cry about a threat to the individual soul. Here you'd find yourself on the wrong side —it's they who stand for the individual, and we just stand for Private 23987, unit in the global strategy."

The Vietminh strategy was above all based on the population. The army was a people's army; it walked among the people; it belonged to the people. The orders from Ho were very simple: the army was to work side by side with the population in the fields, help them with their crops, give them courses in literacy. Above all, the army must honor the population—then and only then would they become one and inseparable, Mao's fish swimming in the water. The passion, the religious fervor and intensity this system produced staggered the Westerner. A French army judge who passed sentence on Vietminh killers, the shock troops of Giap's army, told Lucien Bodard that though he had sent hundreds to their death, not one had ever repudiated the Vietminh.

According to their orders they deny everything, not so much for themselves, as out of a last desperate loyalty expressed in negation. They do not bother to put up a defense, as though they were no longer concerned with their fate—as though they were already beyond material things . . . These Vietminh die splendidly. It is more than courage: it is the highest possible form of detachment. Those who are condemned to death are kept in the little island of Poulo Condore [Con Son], the old penal settlement. Once I had to go there. When I arrived there were 22 men waiting to be executed. They were shut up in special cells . . . When I went into the prison they all began singing their patriotic songs together. They already knew that a squad of legionnaires had disembarked with me to shoot them. I had them stopped for the roll call. Then I said that eleven reprieves had been granted, and eleven refused. So there were eleven of them who were to be executed at once. I went to the office for the usual formalities. I handed out cigarettes. I let them write letters. All this time the men who were about to die were laughing, not in order to insult me, but as though the whole thing amused them. Then for their last minutes they started their singing again . . ."

FOR HO, NOW GUERRILLA LEADER, the wartime years were ones of constant movement. The Vietminh leadership went into the mountains; no two ministers stayed together. Meetings were clandestine: officials came from different directions for these sessions, Ho always the last to arrive.

There was never a betrayal. Security was absolute; the French with airborne troops and planes were not to be permitted to destroy or capture the Vietminh leadership. Ho spent these years working closely with Giap, perfecting the techniques which exploited the potent political and psychological resources of the population and turned them to Vietminh use.

Ho was already the embodiment of the simple man: if others were wary of crossing a stream during a torrential downpour, then Ho himself would find the best place to ford and cross over; when the French bombers appeared, Ho would scurry and hide in the fields like the other peasants; when food supplies were low and starvation seemed a possibility, it was Ho who first cut his own rations to the survival minimum.

The French in 1947 made one last attempt to meet with Ho. They sent Paul Mus, the scholar, through the Vietminh lines and into the jungle to ask Ho to agree to their terms; the terms bordered on unconditional surrender. Mus, understanding this and the psychology of the Vietnamese, knew that it was hopeless. Among other things the French were demanding that the Vietnamese turn over any foreign specialists training Vietminh troops. This would be a betrayal of friends, and Mus knew Ho would never agree. Mus explained the terms; Ho looked at him for a long time. "Monsieur le professeur, you know us very well. If I were to accept this, I would be a coward. The French union is an assemblage of freemen and there can be no place in it for cowards." Then he shook hands with Mus and disappeared into the jungle once more.

FOR EIGHT YEARS the war dragged on. To the French it was always victories, always heavier Vietminh casualties, always winning the war. But always there were more Viets, until slowly it began to dawn on some French officials that this was a war of attrition, and that despite the heavier Vietminh casualty rolls, it was finally the French who were being worn down and exhausted.

It was as Giap and Ho had predicted: the colonial power was tiring of a war which among other things was turning out to be poor economics; Indochina was costing France far more than it was worth. Thirty years earlier in Comintern circles, where others had presented grandiose schemes for toppling Western powers, Ho had written that the way to do it was through long and punishing colonial wars which would sap the very fiber and vitality of the colonial country until both colony and country came apart. He was not far from wrong. That the French could not defeat the Vietminh, the little yellow ones, was a frustrating lesson. Front-line French officers cabled back their reports of losses and of growing Vietminh strength. But the French high command steadfastly refused to listen; it was sure it could win the war. At home, the opposition to the war steadily mounted. To the French command in Hanoi it was those politicians back home who were causing problems, aiding a cowardly enemy who refused to come out and fight.

Finally, as the war dragged on, as the French casualty lists grew longer, the French command decided to set a major trap for the Vietminh. They would position a French garrison in a distant outpost as bait. The Vietminh, who were new to modern warfare, simple people, really, would gather to attack, and as they did, the French would destroy them with artillery and air power. This was the set-piece battle the French wanted so badly.

The name of the outpost was Dienbienphu. The planning was done by men who had underestimated their enemy from the start, who understood neither his talent, his objectives, nor his thinking.

A friend of mine visited the outpost shortly before the battle began. It was in a valley, he noted, surrounded by high peaks in the distance. It gave him a somewhat uneasy feeling—the first rule of warfare is to take the high ground. "Who has the high peaks?" he asked a French officer.

"Who knows?" said the Frenchman, shrugging his shoulders, implicitly indicating that if anyone had them, it was the Vietminh.

"But what if they are there and they have artillery?" my friend insisted.

"They do not have artillery, and even if they did, they would not know how to use it," the Frenchman said.

But they did have artillery. They had carried the pieces up and down mountains, through the monsoons, at night—hundreds of peasants, crawling over the mountain trails like ants, carrying one part after another. This was the Ho Chi Minh trail—not a highway that could be bombed but the willingness of peasants to bear great burdens under terrible conditions. And not only did they have the artillery pieces, they knew how to use them. They had created extraordinary bunkers, perfectly camouflaged, almost impossible to detect from the air.

On March 13, 1954, the battle began. It was, in fact, over before it started. The Vietminh held the high ground and they had the French badly outgunned. The French artillery commander, shouting, "It is my fault! it is my fault!" committed suicide the first night. Day after day the battle wore on as the Vietminh cut the French up. The French garrison made a legendary stand, substituting its own gallantry for the incompetence of its superiors, but all in vain. Fifty-six days later the fort fell. General

Navarre, the French commander, told his other troops: "The defenders of Dienbienphu have written an epic. They have given you a new pride and a new reason to fight. For the struggle of free peoples against slavery does not end today. The fight continues." His men, of course, knew better, as did the rest of the world. The French had been fighting against a revolution and had never realized it until the end. A more accurate description than Navarre's can be found in Jean Larteguy's novel *The Centurions*. A French officer named Glatigny who has just been over-run and defeated at Dienbienphu sees his enemy counter-part for the first time:

> No canvas shoes on his feet and his toes wriggled voluptu-ously in the warm mud of the shelter. Glatigny's reaction was that of a regular officer. He could not believe that this nha que squatting on his haunches and smoking foul tobacco was like him, a battalion commander with the same rank and the same responsibilities as his own. This was one of the officers of the 308th Division, the best unit in the People's Army. It was this peasant from the paddy-fields who had beaten him, Glatigny, the descendant of one of the great military dynasties of the West, for whom war was a profession and the only purpose in life. . . .

IT WAS OVER. Even the set-piece battle had been lost. Now clearly the Vietminh had all the drive and in-itiative. Each day as the war continued, the French were pushed back farther. At the Geneva Conference, where negotiations had been taking place simultaneously, a curi-ous thing happened. The Vietminh, who seemed to be on their way to taking the whole country, were persuaded by the Russians and the French Communists to settle for a partitioned Vietnam, divided at the Seventeenth Parallel, with the Vietminh taking the North, with elections to be held in 1956.

It was relatively clear why the European Communists were willing to push for this: it was a trade that would keep France out of the European Defense Community. Why the Vietminh was willing to settle is not so clear. Perhaps the Russians persuaded Ho and Giap that America, under the influence of John Foster Dulles, might enter the war if the Communists proved inflexible. Perhaps there was a belief on the part of the Vietminh leaders that the South was such a political sewer and so fragmented that they could succeed in taking it over politically instead of militarily, and avoid further loss of their own blood. So they settled for half a country, perhaps a little bitterly. Nevertheless they consoled themselves that they would easily win the forthcoming nationwide election. For Ho was the man who had liberated the Vietnamese from the French. He was the national hero now, the only one; the country was his. Except for a few upper-class Vietnamese in the South, and part of the Catholic minority, there was no one else in a position of leadership.

Ho rode into Hanoi, not as a conqueror, not at the head of a swaggering conquering army, but in his own typically simple style, in a captured French three-quarter-ton truck. It seemed to be yet another gesture to show the people that it was their victory, their spirit which had won—that he was just one of them. He had triumphed over the French and his revolution was a success; his minority Communist party had taken clear title to the nationalism of the country. At every level in the country, tough Communist peasants—like the *nha que* who had confronted Glatigny —members of the battle-hardened party, would take over the structure of the administration. It was not just a defeat of the French; it was a defeat of the mandarin order.

6

THE AMERICANS ARRIVE: THE SECOND INDOCHINA WAR 1955–1969

"That which is not a total success in Indochina will be a total failure."

Lucien Bodard

". . . THEY DON'T WANT COMMUNISM."

"They want rice," I said, "they don't want to be shot at. They want one day to be much the same as another. They don't want our white skins around telling them what they want."

"If Indo-China goes—"

"I know that record. Siam goes. Malaya goes. Indonesia goes. What does 'go' mean? If I believed in your God and another life, I'd bet my future harp against your golden crown that in five hundred years there may be no New York or London but they'll be growing paddy in these fields, they'll be carrying produce to market on long poles, wearing their pointed hats. The small boys will be sitting on buffaloes. I like the buffaloes, they don't like our smell, the smell of Europeans. And remember—from a buffalo's point of view you are a European too."

"They'll be forced to believe what they are told; they won't be allowed to think for themselves."

"Thoughts are luxury. Do you think the peasant sits

and thinks of God and democracy when he gets inside his mud hut at night?"

"You talk as if the whole country were peasant. What about the educated? Are they going to be happy?"

"Oh no," I said, "we've brought them up in our ideas. We've taught them dangerous games, and that's why we are waiting here, hoping we don't get our own throats cut. We deserve to have them cut. . . ."

—Graham Greene, *The Quiet American*, 1956

PEACE WOULD NOT COME EASILY. In the South, the Americans, fearing an international Communist monolith, worried by Mao's takeover of China, embittered by the Korean war, decided to extend to Asia the policy of containment which had worked so well for them in Western Europe, not realizing that the very forces which had made them successful in Europe—the common Christian heritage and tradition—would work against them in Southeast Asia. Dulles, architect of the policy, did not realize this. Indeed at the time of the Geneva agreement he said that Dienbienphu was "a blessing in disguise—we enter Vietnam without the taint of colonialism." A decade later Bernard Fall, watching the frustration of American combat troops sinking in the Vietnamese quagmire, just as the French had before, wrote, far more prophetically, that the Americans were "dreaming different dreams than the French but walking in the same footsteps."

Dulles could not have been more inaccurate: eight years of revolutionary warfare had divided Vietnam by more than the Seventeenth Parallel. All the most vital and ablest young men had gone over to the Vietminh; it was they who controlled the most powerful and popular forces. Indeed, it was recognition of this fact that caused the Americans to work against holding nationwide elections;

they knew Ho would win easily. At the same time as they were fighting a war, the Vietminh had been forging an operative system—a modern society.

The reverse was true of the South. It was a society made up of people who had either fought for the French or stayed on the sidelines during those most crucial years, men who had fought against their country, done nothing for it, or profiteered during its war for independence. The Americans chose Ngo Dinh Diem to be the leader of their state. He was a symbolic choice: a Catholic in a Buddhist country, a central Vietnamese in the South, a mandarin in a land which had just been swept by revolutionary forces that left mandarin ways smashed in their wake. He was the wrong man for Vietnam but the right man for the Americans: he was at once anti-French and anti-Communist. He was the perfect emblem of an attempt to turn back the clock, a Western-oriented leader in a country which had just gone through an anti-Western revolution. Graham Greene wrote prophetically of him as he took over in 1955: "One pictured him sitting there in the Norodom Palace, sitting with his blank brown gaze, incorruptible, obstinate, ill-advised, going to his weekly confession, bolstered up by his belief that God is always on the Catholic side, waiting for a miracle. The name I would write under his portrait is Patriot Ruined by the West."

Diem, of course, had little political base (except for his family—how much a relic of the Vietnamese past that was), and he took over a hopelessly fragmented society. "The thing you must remember about politicians in the South," a South Vietnamese told me in 1967, "is that they hate each other very much because that is traditional, but they also hate themselves very much for not having fought against the French. There are—how do you say it?—considerable psychological problems here." Diem's base was composed of the Americans, his own considerable police powers, and a handful of anti-Communist nationalists. Suspicious of the others, and hearing of endless plotting around him in the Vietnamese tradition, Diem soon relied more and more on his police powers. This drove out some of his remaining allies, which made him even more suspicious, which in turn drove out even more allies and made him even more suspicious. Soon it was just him and his family. Four years into his rule, Diem who had been hailed in the West as a miracle man simply for lasting out the first two years, found that his already narrow political base was shrinking rather than expanding.

DIEM AND THE AMERICANS had blocked elections in 1956 and Diem had carried out massive arrests against all his political opponents, particularly anyone who had fought with the Vietminh. It was typical of the political schizophrenia of the South that no book which told about the successful war against the French could be published during the Diem years, that almost no Vietnamese who had ever been with the Vietminh could work for the Americans or the government, whereas anyone who had fought for the French could hold whatever job he wanted —he was safer.

In 1959 the second part of the Indochina war started. It was fought by Southerners in the South. Some of them, members of the Vietminh, had gone to the North in 1954, been trained there and then infiltrated their way back. The new Communist force was called the Vietcong, although it was the direct descendant of the Vietminh. Most observers believe that the decision to start the war was made in Hanoi, and that the pace, strategy and orchestration was largely set in the North. It was in all its essential elements a continuation of the first war. The only people who failed to perceive this were the highly placed Americans running the war; because of their own background, and because of political expediency, they chose to see it more as a continuation of the Korean experience, an essentially conventional war. Indeed at first they trained the South Vietnamese army in classic conventional infantry tactics rather than guerrilla tactics. Even after they finally perceived the guerrilla nature of the war, they conveniently managed to separate it from its political roots, as if the military operation were an end in itself.

There were just a few differences from the French war to allow for new realities: the propaganda emphasis, rather than being against the French and the colonialists, was now on locally important issues—more stress was placed on the failure of land reform, for example. Diem—fortunately for the Vietminh—had gone into the rich delta areas where in the 1950s the Vietminh had distributed the land to the peasants, taken the land back from them and returned it to its original owners. It was not that he particularly liked the landowning class—if anything he was more sympathetic to the peasants. The explanation was even more painful: he had a mandarin's notion of right and wrong, and this illegal distribution offended his moral sense.

To Ho there was little doubt that the second war would be a success too. No matter that the superpower America was aiding the South; he realized that the Saigon government had no base of popular support, that its defeat would only be a matter of time and suffering. His was a modern revolutionary state; that in the South was a feudal, anachronistic one. He told Bernard Fall in 1962: "Sir, you have studied us for ten years, you have written about the Indochina war. It took us eight years of bitter fighting to defeat you French in Indochina. Now the Diem regime is well armed and helped by many Americans. The Americans are stronger than the French. It might take ten years, but our heroic compatriots in the South will defeat them in the end. . . . I think the Americans greatly underestimate the determination of the Vietnamese people. The Vietnamese people have always shown great determination when faced with an invader."

The confidence was clearly there; Ho knew his side had all the dynamism and the nationalism. Fall mentioned the American aid—the Americans had sent 18,000 troops and six helicopter companies to help Saigon. Pham Van Dong (with Ho at the interview) was still sure of success:

"Diem is unpopular and the more unpopular he is, the more American aid he will need to remain in power. And the more American aid he gets, the more of an American puppet he'll look and the less likely he is to regain popularity."

"That sounds pretty much like a vicious circle, doesn't it?" interjected Fall.

"No sir," said Dong, with a little laugh, "it is a downward spiral."

In Hanoi, Ho himself was secure. Though Westerners would write from time to time of rivalries within the leadership, Ho's very presence seemed to smooth them over. When Sainteny had once asked Ho about the threat from the angry young turks like Truong Chinh and Giap, Ho had said, "What could they possibly do without me? It was I who made them." Right after the war, gossip had intensified because the offices of Prime Minister and Head of State which Ho had held jointly were separated—did this mean Ho was through, doddering, replaced by the young men? In 1956 they realized how much they needed him. The party's harsh land-reform program led to a major peasant rebellion in Ho's own province. The regime brutally repressed it, and in consequence for the first time was in disfavor with the population. It was to Ho that the party turned. He took over as Party Secretary, Truong Chinh was made the scapegoat; errors in handling the rebellion were publicly admitted. The crisis passed. His own popularity was the party's greatest asset.

He was, if anything, more genial and confident than ever, sure of himself, sure of his relationship to history. (He teased Bernard Fall when he claimed that his wife had sketched Ho: "Where? Where? Providing she's got my goatee right. Providing the goatee looks all right. Mmm, yes, that is very good. That looks very much like me," and gave Fall a flower for his wife.) And he was sure of his relationship with the party and his people, so that he could in 1960 listen to the National Assembly debating a new constitution and finally comment: "Well, if you want my opinion, I consider Clause A incomprehensible, Clause B inexplicable, Clause C a bit naïve . . ." This brought on great roars of laughter. "Oh, so you're laughing. In that case I've won my point. One has only to achieve such an atmosphere and half one's problems are solved . . ."

THE SPIRAL that Pham Van Dong talked about continued downward. In 1962, under President Kennedy, America armed the South Vietnamese with the best of American weapons, helicopters, jet fighters, motorized riverboats, armed personnel carriers (to cross the paddies at rice-harvest time), the most modern radio equipment. The Americans were very optimistic (the two greatest exports of South Vietnam in the 1960s were anti-Communism and American optimism) because their modern weaponry seemed so overpowering against the ill-armed, poorly clad Vietcong units. But it meant simply that the Vietcong captured better weapons. Again the Vietcong touched on powerful latent forces: the abundant misery of the population.*

The combination of indigenous grievances with the Vietcong's capacity to exploit them made the outcome inevitable. The Vietcong, modern in thought but poorly equipped, fought at night and in the jungles; the ARVN (South Vietnamese army), modern in equipment, was afraid of the night and the bush. The Vietcong was a product of the new society. Its officers were peasant-born, with restless aspirations to power, reacting against age-old grievances, taking advantage of the powerful new egalitarian trends sweeping the world. Vietcong officers had a sense of cause and duty.

The ARVN officer corps was a reflection of existing privilege, neo-mandarin, upper-class, urban, contemptuous of the peasants. It was virtually impossible for anyone who had fought against the French in the first war to be allowed to fight for Saigon now; it was almost equally impossible for anyone of peasant origin to become an ARVN officer. And who were these generals that the Americans liked so much, with their crew cuts and their American slang? They were former French corporals. The

* An American intelligence officer interrogating a Vietcong soldier understood part of the reason for their success. "Tell me about your background," he said. The soldier replied: "I was the eighth of ten children and we were very poor. We had no land of our own. I tended ducks for other people. We were moved around a great deal. Once I tried to save money and buy a flock of ducks to raise for myself, but I failed. I never married. Once I fell in love with a village girl, but I was so ashamed of my status that I did not declare my love to her." "Were you angry at society because of this?" the American asked. "I thought if we were poor it was our own fault. I told myself that probably my poverty was the result of some terrible acts of my ancestors. I was sad, but not angry."

result was inevitable: despite all the massive American aid, despite the fact that for Hanoi and for Peking and Moscow it was a shoestring war, the Vietcong turned the tide against the ARVN in mid-1963, capturing the better weapons to use against Saigon. In late 1963 the Diem government collapsed and he was assassinated. By 1964 the ARVN had been defeated by an indigenous peasant army. It was just as Ho had predicted.

WHEN THE KENNEDY COMMITMENT to help South Vietnam help itself failed in 1964, the Americans were caught between two alternatives: either they could withdraw their forces and seek a neutralized (and eventually Communist) Vietnam or they could go ahead with a full escalation. Their own pride and vanity—even manhood—were at stake, just as those of the French had been two decades before. At a cocktail party in Washington someone mentioned that victory might take the Americans as long as it had the British in Malaya—eight years. "We are *not* the British," a high American military official answered archly. What had happened to the French would not happen to them; they were, after all, a mighty power with a mighty air force, whereas the French had been a second-rate power coming out of World War II virtually without air power. Besides, the Americans felt morally superior to the French; like John Foster Dulles they were sure they had no taint of colonialism. Thus in February 1965 they decided to bomb the North and shortly afterward to send combat troops to South Vietnam, plunging ahead into the same political problems the French had faced.

Once more the issue of Communist or non-Communist was dwarfed in Vietnamese eyes; the issue of Vietnamese or non-Vietnamese dominated instead. The Americans, as

Fall had said, would be walking more in French footsteps than they realized.

The machinery which Ho and Giap had set up so effectively during the first war continued to function as effectively in the second, with a few adjustments to account for the greater American air power. For instance, Giap learned how to counter American air power by joining the battle so closely that American planes would kill Americans as well. But the style was the same—frustrate the enemy, wear them out, bog them down in the quagmire make victory elusive, make for the Americans the only tangible symbol of the war their own casualty lists. Like the French, the Americans could control only the land they stood on because, though they had total military superiority, the other side had total political superiority—it controlled the population.

Every American commander could report after every battle that, despite his losses, five, six, eight, ten times as many of the enemy had been killed—and no one would dispute him, least of all Giap and Ho. Yet the Vietcong kept coming. Each year the Americans started out with an estimate of enemy in the country; if it was, say, 75,000, that year they might kill 85,000, only to find that at the end of the year there were 90,000. They were fighting the birth rate of the nation. Like the French they could fight bravely, they could kill and they could die—but the enemy kept coming; there was always more of him.

Lucien Bodard once wrote simple but prophetic words: that which is not a total success in Indochina will be a total failure. The Americans learned this too. They thought it would be a short war, but year after year victory remained elusive. In the long painful days of 1968 and 1969 the American government began to learn this most difficult lesson of all about intervention in Vietnam. But it was not a lesson a great superpower learns readily. In 1967 Lyndon Johnson, the restless powerhouse of a President, had met with his Vietnamese overlord, Air Marshal Nguyen Cao Ky, a fighter pilot. (What could be more American and less Vietnamese in a country where people still lived among the water buffalo than a leader whose base of power was a jet plane? It was a symbol of his lack of roots.) Carried away by the excitement and euphoria of the occasion—charts everywhere, all showing success, all showing a beaten enemy—Johnson told Ky, Hurry up and win the war, bring those coonskins back. Like so many others before him, he thought victory was near; like so many others, he was wrong.

In February 1968, Vo Nguyen Giap launched what was later called the Tet offensive, which punctured overnight the official American illusion of an exhausted enemy and an imminent American military victory. He used the strategy of fighting in the cities rather than the countryside. This limited the use of American air power. It also advanced the Vietminh political struggle by forcing the use of air power against Vietnamese civilians. After the offensive, an American major, looking at the town of Ben Tre, spoke the final epitaph for the American effort: "We had to destroy the town to save it."

Ho was also waging political warfare on another front: it was an American election year and the Tet offensive thus would have a special import for Americans. By fighting in the cities, his forces had given American news cameramen something to shoot day after day. For more than two weeks Americans watched on their television sets as reports of the Tet struggle came home: clearly only American air power and artillery finally drove the North Vietnamese and Vietcong troops from the cities. For the first time the Vietcong and North Vietnamese courage and persistence became tangible to viewing Americans. The result was predictable. Lyndon Johnson, who had won by a landslide in 1964 (who had in 1965 boasted to White House intimates about what he had done to Ho: "I just cut his p - - - - off"), decided not to run again, his Great Society stillborn, his ambition and hope for a historic Presidency mired in the rice paddies of Vietnam —one more foolish Westerner who, in the words of reporter Neil Sheehan, had lost his reputation to Ho Chi Minh.

ON SEPTEMBER 3, 1969, Ho Chi Minh, peasant-born, most of his life an outlaw from the world around him, died. The war was continuing much as he would have predicted. A new American President, still unable to come to terms with that most bitter lesson for Westerners, the fact that if you have not defeated guerrillas you have lost to them, was bogged down in the war. He was promising to disengage while at the same time boasting to his countrymen that they would not lose the war, and the conflict was beginning to cost him control of his own country. The domestic forces which Vietnam had helped create now tore at the very fabric of American society, and Ho, who more than forty years before had said that the way to weaken the West was through colonial wars, would have taken a prophet's pleasure in his prediction. In Vietnam, Ho's forces firmly controlled half the country and it seemed only a matter of time before they would take power nationwide. American officials who a few short years earlier had talked glibly about Hanoi's threshold of pain—how much bombing, how many troops it would take to reach it—were now finding that their own threshold of pain was lower. ("And how long do you Americans want to fight, Mr. Salisbury?" Pham Van Dong asked Harrison Salisbury of *The New York Times* in 1967. "One year, two years, three years, five years, ten years, twenty years . . . we will be glad to accommodate you.")

With Ho's death, power was transferred in Hanoi without any crisis; his goals had always been his people's goals, so there was no readjustment of his vision to be made. Judged by his impact on his own poor country, his life was an extraordinary success and a vindication; he was the greatest patriot of his people in this century. But his impact was far greater than this. In Europe his victory had helped teach the French that a colonial era had come to an end, and thus France would liquidate its sub-Sahara African empire without a shot fired. And in the United States, his impact was even greater. Political leaders like Robert Kennedy, who had begun the decade convinced that America had a right, indeed a duty, to fight brush-fire wars in underdeveloped nations around the world, would change their minds and not only turn against the war, but talk of a new definition of American foreign policy, emphasizing now the limits of power, saying that the United States cannot be the policeman of the world. The war thus hastened the end of two decades of American foreign policy based upon the sole guiding principle of anti-Communism.

The combination of the war and domestic racial failures was having an even deeper effect upon young educated Americans (many of whom in 1970 would go to their antiwar rallies shouting, Ho, Ho, Ho Chi Minh). To a remarkable degree it changed their sense of values: traditional armed force was now in their eyes a sign of weakness, simple peasant resistance a strength; the contemporary who followed his conscience and refused to serve in Vietnam became a hero, instead of the young man who fought and won his nation's highest medals.

After Richard Nixon ordered the attack on the base camps in Cambodia in May 1970, the disaffection of the young indeed threatened the stability of the society. Joseph Alsop, a hawk columnist, was moved to a unique exchange of letters with Senator Edward Kennedy. Alsop deplored the "political lunacy" of the young in "passionately demonstrating against your own country's successes on the battlefield," and said that only Kennedy could bring the young to their senses. To which Kennedy, political heir of two brothers who had helped initiate the war, wrote, "We are a nation constantly being reborn, and we can thank our God that those newly arrived in our society will not casually accept the views and presumptions of their fathers, much less their errors. They do not protest their 'country's successes on the battlefield,' doubtful as those successes may be; they protest the very existence of the battlefield, for it has no place in their vision of the country that is to be theirs. And I support them in that."

IN HIS LIFETIME Ho had not only liberated his own country and changed the course of colonial rule in both Africa and Asia, he had done something even more remarkable; he had touched the culture and the soul of his enemy. For goat-bearded, Mongoloid-Trotsky, tubercular agitator Ho Chi Minh, it had been a full life.

Bibliography

Bodard, Lucien, *The Quicksand War*. Boston: Little Brown; Published by Atlantic Monthly Press, 1967.

Buttinger, Joseph, *Vietnam: A Dragon Embattled*, Volumes 1 and 2. New York: Praeger, 1967.

De Antonio, Emile, *The Year of the Pig* (a film, 1969).

Fall, Bernard, "Ho Chi Minh, Like It or Not." New York: *Esquire* magazine, November 1967.

Fall, Bernard, *Ho Chi Minh on Revolution*. New York: Praeger, 1967.

Greene, Graham, *The Quiet American*. New York: Viking, 1956.

Isaacs, Harold, *No Peace for Asia*. New York: Macmillan, 1947.

Lacouture, Jean, *Ho Chi Minh*. New York: Random House, 1968.

McAlister, John, *The Origins of Revolution*. New York: Alfred A. Knopf, 1969.

McAlister, John, and Mus, Paul, *The Vietnamese and Their Revolution*. New York: Harper & Row, 1970.

Shaplen, Robert, *The Lost Revolution: The U.S. in Vietnam*. New York: Harper & Row, 1965.

ABOUT THE AUTHOR

David Halberstam was twenty-eight years old when he went to Vietnam as a reporter for the New York Times in 1962. His early pessimistic dispatches for the Times won him a Pulitzer prize in 1964. His books on Vietnam include The Making of a Quagmire, One Very Hot Day, *and the landmark political study,* The Best and the Brightest. *In* Ho, *Mr. Halberstam has combined a firsthand knowledge of Asia with his unique abilities as a political reporter. His most recent book is* The Reckoning, *a story of the Japanese challenge to American corporations.*